THE UNAUTHORIZED B...

TYSON FURY
Fighting Shadows

By the acclaimed author of *"Bruce Lee: Fighting Spirit"*
Bruce Thomas

TYSON FURY

Fighting Shadows

Other books by Bruce Thomas:

Bruce Lee: Fighting Spirit

Bruce Lee: Complete Teachings

Rough Notes

For everyone facing a challenge

© 2019 Bruce Thomas

The right of Bruce Thomas to be identified as the author of this work has been asserted by him in accordance with the Copyright, Designs and Patents Act of 1988.

All rights reserved.

Except for the purposes of review, no part of this publication may be reproduced, stored in a retrieval system, or transmitted in any form by any means electronic, mechanical, photocopying, recording or otherwise, without the prior permission of the copyright holder.

Rough Notes Press

Contents

1	Born Fighter	13
2	Through the Ranks	29
3	Shadow Boxing	36
4	Furious	43
5	Fury v Klitschko	53
6	Gathering Moss	80
7	*He's Back!*	105
8	Fighting Weight	122
9	The First Step	136
10	Future Prospect	146
11	Good Business	162
12	Fury v Wilder	172

I'd like people to get to know the real Tyson Fury — behind all the bravado, behind all the cheek, behind the big person trying to sell fights and sell tickets, and create controversy and interest.

* * *

I'm the unofficial ambassador for mental health in sport. It's my biggest goal. That's my only calling card. That's the reason I'm back — it's to show people that are living in darkness that there is light at the end of the tunnel.

Round 1

Born Fighter

TYSON LUKE FURY WAS BORN ON 12 AUGUST 1988 IN THE Wythenshawe district of Manchester and raised there in a family of Irish travellers. He identifies strongly with this heritage. In the days before political correctness reared its head, 'travellers' were known with more authenticity, more accuracy, and perhaps even more dignity, as gypsies. Tyson is a distant relative of self-styled King of the Gypsies, Bartley Gorman — hence Fury's own nickname, Gypsy King. The Fury family consider themselves to be of Romany extraction, gifted with 'second sight', and with a strong belief in the supernatural.

'Fury' is a derivation of the Gaelic, *Ó Fiodhabhra*. Tyson's father John's side of the family are Catholics from Galway. His mother, Amber, a Belfast protestant, had fourteen pregnancies, but only four children survived — all boys. In

1997, daughter Ramona was born two days before Christmas but died within days — an experience, says Fury, who was just nine at the time, which has stayed with him.

Tyson Fury is the kind of name that a scriptwriter would come up with for a movie about a heavyweight champion, but it's no professional stage name. He was christened Tyson after Mike Tyson, the then world champion because, from day one, John Fury believed it was his son's destiny to also become the world heavyweight boxing champion. This was something more than a simple leap of faith — the boy had been born extremely premature and barely survived his first few days. He was kept alive only by John massaging his heart with the tip of his finger.

John Fury:

His mother had to go in to the hospital early because of some pains. The baby wasn't due for another eight or nine weeks. About three in the morning, I got a phone call from the doctors.

They said, 'He's being born.'

I said, 'He ain't due.'

They said, 'Unforeseen complications — we can only hope for the best.'

So he was born and taken to the special care unit. He was only about a pound and a half in weight. I put him in the palm of my hand and looked at him.

The doctor looked at me and I said, 'Miracles do happen. He'll live. He'll be champion of the world. His name's Tyson – forget about the Mike. I believe in fate. He's here to do a job. He's got the best boxer name ever, let's be honest.'

'I hope things work out for you,' said the doctor.

Tyson Fury:
When I was born I weighed one pound. I died three times. I was born at seven months' ...premature. The doctor said to my Dad, 'Well, he's here, but he's not very strong ...he's not very big.' My dad went to pick me up in his hands, and he looked at me and went, 'He'll do.' I made up for it in the meantime.

Fury grew up in Styal, near Wilmslow, and left school at the age of eleven to join his father, John, and three brothers tarmacking roads, having already started boxing at the age of ten. John won eight of his own thirteen licensed fights, but there were a lot more bare-knuckle bouts where he earned the majority of his prizemoney.

A bare-knuckle fight — a fist fight — could happen in a cold, wet car park at the back of a remote pub on the Moors — or in an abandoned warehouse in some Northern town like Bolton. Details were rarely revealed to outsiders. Sometimes it might be a prize fight where purses could reach £50,000. At other times it might be a family argument that was being settled — or the latest instalment of a feud that went back generations.

There might be a couple of three-minute rounds, or half an hour of slugging it out, with no ring and no ropes. Maybe there'd be a referee, or simply a representative from each of the warring families. The only certainty was that there'd be blood.

As far back as he could remember the young Tyson went everywhere with his father — sitting on an upturned bucket watching — watching everything — taking it all in. As quickly as he learned to walk, he was already steeped in boxing. Tyson Fury was already a boxer before he knew he could be anything different. Fury acknowledges that all the bareknuckle stuff goes on but insists he's never wanted any part of it.

> *I stay away from all that. I don't go to travellers' fairs and horse-racing dos. Or anywhere that people get drunk and challenge me to a fight. Me being a boxer, they get a few beers inside them and they think they're Mike Tyson and Muhammad Ali rolled into one and start brawling. I'd get me licence taken off me if I got involved. I'm not a troublesome person. I've never had a fight outside the ring in me life.*
>
> *Boxing is a key element of the travelling culture. In other cultures little kids will kick a ball about; we're punching hands. When we have a dispute we're not supposed to go to the police, we're supposed take our shirts off, go outside and sort it out with fisticuffs. To be a good fighting man is one of the best things you can ever be in life.*

The entire Fury family is steeped in a long history in boxing. Three of Tyson Fury's cousins are boxers — the Irish former WBO middleweight champion, Andy Lee; the former British light-heavyweight champion, Hosea Burton; and the English heavyweight champion, Hughie Fury. It was his father John who inspired Tyson to box and who acted as his first trainer. But at the same time, for a substantial period and to make sure Tyson was committed, John Fury refused to drive his son to the gym so that he was forced to make his own way. Often, he simply made the long walk there.

> *My brother Shane was my first sparring partner. We grew up together playing boxing and sparring each other constantly. We had tea towels, dishcloths, wrapped around our hands. We used to spar in the kitchen. At the time we would only find one pair of gloves in the house. I don't know why – they were my Dad's old gloves from when he used to train. They were all stinky and sweaty and we used to have one glove each and one tea towel each and we used to spar full on — plates going everywhere. Even when we weren't playing, we'd design world championship boxing kits.*

Shane Fury:
> Before the boxing, Tyson was always a skinny little boy — very quiet, placid, and shy. As he got older and started boxing he put weight on and grew in confidence around that — because he was so good from the word 'go'.

Tyson Fury claims he doesn't recall when he threw his first punch:

> *I've been throwing punches since I was in the womb ...When I first laced on gloves ... every day since then ... not for one day did I doubt the fact that I'd be heavyweight champion of the world. Nobody could handle me — from that day to this. I was fighting British champions when I was fifteen-years-old and they couldn't handle me. I always knew I had something better than the next man.*

Tyson had no formal education, but he was still the smartest in the house, good at arithmetic and English, according to his father. He would write stories in which he pictured himself as a world champion.

'My reading wasn't very good,' says John Fury. 'I would get letters and ask him, "What does this mean?" and he would tell me.

The boy also spent time in Morecambe with his uncle, Hughie — where he slept in a trailer at the back of the house and trained in an old ring that had been brought over from Dundalk — along with some rusty old weights that were found in the same shed — in the family's long-haul van, via the Belfast –Heysham ferry.

> *I loved every minute of it. I just wanted to get better and learn. I was like a sponge soaking everything up. I didn't want to be a big stiff with my hands up around my face, walking forward. I wanted to slip*

and slide and be a boxer. I wanted American style with European conditioning. And that's what I eventually got.

* * *

Coaches at Jimmy Egan's Boxing Academy, in Wythenshawe, still remember vividly where it all began for Tyson Fury. Their gym is where the six-foot-plus, fourteen-year-old would lace up a proper pair of boxing gloves. Multiple punch bags lined the front of the small room — with inspirational quotes from Muhammad Ali and Mike Tyson across the walls. Among them, now, is an image of Fury with a quote that reads, 'I was made by God, but trained at Jimmy Egan's'. It was here that the young Fury was moulded into a national amateur champion. Jimmy Egan's son Steve reflects on those early days...

> I wouldn't say he was talented — just a gangly lad — just a big lad, with fast hands. But he wasn't like most learners who come in. He was trying the odd body shot and I thought, 'That's good for a big lad.' And you think about what you've done with good lads and think, 'If I can put that in him, how good is he going to be?' I thought, 'He's always going to be a heavyweight. Look at the size of him.' So the first day I saw him I said to him, 'Heavyweight Champion of the World'.

But after the happy memories of training the gym's most successful boxer there come hints of regret. Egan revealed that he gave up work so that he could train Fury full-time because of the potential he saw...

> I didn't work for two years at one stage. I tried working part-time but my boss let me go and I lost my job. I made the sacrifice because I knew he could be world champion. I know my dad wasn't here then, but the gym's in my dad's name, it's our gym and our ethos.

When asked why the two drifted apart, Egan struggled for words, understandably feeling disappointed that the gym that played a key role in Fury's development isn't generally recognised...

> I don't know. Maybe he just wanted to go in a different direction. What can you say? I wanted him to stay with me ... He doesn't shout it from the rooftops that he trained here, does he? Not a lot of people know. Everyone in the amateur boxing game knows he trained here, but in the pros and in the general public, not many people know. It's not mentioned that much, it'd be nice. He doesn't say he's from Jimmy Egan's.

* * *

As a junior amateur, Fury was ranked World #3 and represented both Ireland and England. At first, he fought out of the Holy Family Boxing Club, in Belfast, in the North, and later switched to the Smithboro Club, in Monaghan, in the Republic. In 2006, he won bronze at the Amateur Youth World Boxing Championships — and in the same year, represented Jimmy Egan's Boxing Academy in England, where he took part in the Senior National Championships. In 2007, in an international competition against an experienced Polish team Fury won both of his bouts. In a later Irish match against a US team he won his bout by KO.

But Fury was forced to withdraw from the Irish National Championships after a protest regarding his eligibility. He later had problems in gaining dual citizenship because, in the 1960s, his father's birth in Galway hadn't been officially recorded with the State. At that time travellers' births were only recorded through baptism with the Church.

Tyson Fury has claimed that, by the age of eighteen, he'd accumulated over £120,000 in cash — most of which he lost in the casinos, as he already had he eyes on greater fortunes. At the age of twenty, he became national ABA champion. Prior to the 2008 Beijing Olympics, Tyson Fury and David Price were seen as the two outstanding candidates to represent the Team GB boxing. Having had a longer amateur career, it was Price who got the nod. Fury was upset, not so much at not going, but at not actually being a chance to go — not being given an opportunity to prove himself as the best choice.

I never wanted be an amateur. To me, amateur boxing was something I had to do to turn professional. I was never interested in boxing for a plastic cup ...ever. I always wanted to be world heavyweight champion, professional. Anything less was a failure in my eyes. The GB team asked me to stick around for the London 2012 Olympics, but I don't like waiting for things. Strike while the iron is hot!

Team Fury believes that Tyson lost out to Price for both the Commonwealth and Olympic Games simply because of prejudice. When Fury and his father travelled to Ireland to meet with the selectors, they allegedly learned that the selectors had already been informed by the British Boxing Board of Control that if Tyson was selected then, all ties between the two bodies would be severed. It was a small, but crucial, event that set the tone for the underlying 'battle' that Tyson Fury would feel throughout his entire career.

On 6 December 2008, Tyson Fury made his professional debut in Nottingham — on the undercard of Carl Froch v Jean Pascal — against the Hungarian fighter, Bela Gyongyosi. Fury won by a TKO in Round 1 with a smart head-body combination. By July 2009, Fury had won his first six fights in the space of just seven months — all by KO — all within four rounds. He'd also found the time to get married.

Tyson Fury married his teenage sweetheart, Paris Mullroy, in November 2008. By all accounts the early stages of their relationship were a little shaky. After being set up with him by a relative, Tyson wasn't quite what she was expecting.

> I was first introduced to Tyson by his Auntie Theresa. She's known as the matchmaker in the family. She said to Tyson, 'Come and meet this young lady.' I lifted my head and was expecting to see someone at eye level

because I'm not that small myself — I'm five foot nine. I remember thinking, 'Who's this old man you're introducing me to?' He had a full beard, and was built like a machine. I thought, 'You're not a young boy— I'm off! — you've introduced me to an old man.'

But the two met again at Paris' 16th birthday party, which was the moment they began to be attracted to each other.

Tyson was quite shy, he didn't speak a lot. The only thing I remember him saying was, "You look like a Cindy doll" — and that upset me because Sindy is a second-rate Barbie. I said, 'At least call me a Barbie!' We ended up going out a few times, but to us 'going out' meant that you go on dates and you see each other, but you don't kiss, you don't cuddle, you don't do anything else. We'd go to the cinema and ice skating every weekend. We were watching *King Kong* at the cinema when I finally said, 'Yeah, I'll be your girlfriend.' We were very innocent kids. He was my first love. I'd never even kissed anyone, and I was thinking, 'Now I've said that, he's gonna kiss me in a minute.' After an hour of feeling awkward he still hadn't kissed me. In the end I burst out laughing. I said, 'I can't kiss you …because I don't know what to do either!'

Even after we got engaged, Tyson would sleep in a caravan at my parents' home, while I slept inside the house. We didn't sleep together until after we got married. That's the travellers' way.'

It was a gypsy wedding – but not a big fat one.

You wouldn't have 'big fat Pakistani weddings' or 'big fat Black weddings'. It's discrimination and it's very offensive. There are idiots out there like the people on those programmes, but you can find the good and bad in all walks of life. If you go to Wythenshawe, where I was brought up, it's not like that.

Paris Fury explains the Gypsy lifestyle:

You are what you are. It's a way of life and is like being Asian or Black or Jewish. *My Big Fat Gypsy Wedding* gave a very bad image of what travellers are like and most travellers are not like that, just a very small minority. People from a travelling background have big families and it's quite old-fashioned and everyone looks out for each other. It is like a community.

Paris is also from travelling stock, but Fury insists he was free to marry outside the community had he wished ...though some of his views on women would hardly be endorsed by feminists.

She's nice-looking and a nice person. She does a lot of housework and cleaning and cooks for me five times a day. She looks after me really well. A woman's a woman and she's there to be loved and cook some food and have some kids, not to get involved in men's business. I know your general public woman wouldn't put up with it because she would want to be involved. She'd want a pair of balls. We don't agree with that.

Fury sounded genuinely amazed when he described all the cooking and washing he had to do in a training camp, as if he's somehow stumbled upon unequivocal proof of womankind's true calling.

> *These women, they really do deserve a lot of respect. I had to sack myself from doing the washing — I couldn't keep on top of it.*

It is worth adding that, in reality, Tyson Fury sees a lot more in Paris than most people credit. As is often the case, it is 'the woman at home' that holds it all together. That their marriage endured is due to the consistency and stability that she has come to offer his impulsiveness and volatility. She has become his true counsel — a counsel that, more than once, would prove invaluable to him.

Round 2

Through the Ranks

O N 11 SEPTEMBER 2009, TYSON FURY FOUGHT JOHN MC Dermott for the English heavyweight title. After fighting the full ten rounds, Fury won on the referee's points' decision. But this decision was far from accepted by everyone. It was a close fight, and seemingly a lot of people had unofficially scored the fight in favour of McDermott. *The Guardian's* Kevin Mitchell didn't pull any punches...

> There are bad decisions in boxing and there are monumental errors - such as the diabolical verdict Terry O'Connor handed down to John McDermott in Brentwood on Friday night when Tyson Fury clearly got away with a robbery of the highway variety.

Fury, a bankable prospect, keeps his slate clean and will be marketed accordingly. It did him no good, though, to declare afterwards he thought he was a deserved winner — especially when his corner could be heard telling him before he went out for the final round that he was behind on points

The British Boxing Board of Control were discussing the controversy today. They will announce their findings tomorrow. If they are in any way moved by the injustice, they will ban O'Connor for at least six months and order a rematch. I honestly cannot remember a worse decision in the sport.

[O'Connor] read the fight poorly throughout, failing to see the steady, if dull, work McDermott was doing, and crediting Fury with points for eye-catching flurries. The 1/6 favourite [Fury] couldn't get going, and should have paid the price. He boxed in spurts against an unfashionable opponent who'd trained his backside off for a contest that meant everything to him. This wasn't just a fight for the English heavyweight title; it was for bragging rights between two proud members of the travelling community.

A rematch is obviously the next step — and Fury will not box as poorly again. But, if he doesn't work off that spare tyre — if he doesn't get serious about his trade — he will throw away a very promising career. And next time, you can bet on McDermott being even more determined to set things right.

Fury himself said later that neither the TV commentary, nor the images, showed the power and effect of the punches he was landing, and had favoured McDermott's performance instead. He added that he'd been disappointed with his own performance because he felt that he'd 'over-trained.' But with this slight blip in his smooth progress through the ranks out of the way, Fury soon went on to gain two further victories — against Tomas Mrazek and Hans-Joerg Blasko.

* * *

The rematch with John McDermott took place on 25 June 2010. This time there was no controversy. It wasn't what you'd call a stylish victory — with both fighters suffering from the sweltering heat inside the venue — but Fury showed guts, strength, and resolve.

He boxed well in the opening round, keeping McDermott at bay with his long jab, before landing two telling right crosses. In the 2nd, Fury took a heavy right hook and, as the fight progressed, McDermott began to produce better work behind his jab. His best round was the 6th, when he landed a heavy right hook. But Fury was responding in kind.

The 21-year-old Fury was deducted a point in the 7th for repeated holding. He'd come into the fight at a career-high 270 pounds — and was said to have had a short training camp in which he'd sparred no more than ten rounds — all of which were factors contributing to Fury's stamina. Both fighters looked more in danger of dropping from heat exhaustion than from a blow.

But a decisive barrage dropped McDermott close to the end of the round. It was the first time in his 32-fight career that McDermott had been down. As he took a left and a right to the head, his legs gave out on him. He made it up and got to his corner, but at the start of the next round his legs still hadn't come back. A short chopping right put him back on the canvas in the 9th. In the next exchange he went down again, only to stagger to his feet on the ten count.

Because of the previous controversy, this time there were three judges. Going into the 9th round, they all had the contest scored 77-73 in favour of Fury.

It was a key fight in Fury's career, and one in which he visibly went up a level to secure the vacant English heavyweight title and so move a step closer to a shot at the British heavyweight belt. But, among the pundits, there were still detractors.

> He is in line for a shot at British champ, Derek Chisora, which would be an awful fight for him right now. Chisora is no world-beater, but he's aggressive, very strong, and just too much man for Fury at this stage. If Tyson and his team are smart, they'll forget about everyone else's expectations and start refining the big man's game some. He's so young that he's still awkward with his own body, and I honestly see him leaving himself so wide open that a fighter like Chisora would take his head off in short and brutal fashion. Realistically, he needs a couple more years seasoning, but with the hype and the TV money waiting for him,

he might not get it. Two life-and-death struggles with McDermott do not mean he's ready for another step up just yet.

But after a further three victories — two 8th-round points decisions over the American fighters, Rich Power and Zack Page, and a 5th-round knockout of the Brazilian, Marcelo Luis Nacimento — a year later, Tyson Fury took on Dereck Chisora.

* * *

On 23 July 2011, at Wembley Arena in London, Tyson Fury fought Dereck Chisora for the British and Commonwealth heavyweight titles. Although Chisora was aged 27, and Fury just 22, both men went into the fight with a record of 14 wins and 0 defeats. Despite Fury's superior physical condition and reach, Chisora started as the favourite.

Fury started the fight on the front foot, looking sharper than Chisora, who looked exactly like a boxer who hadn't fought for nearly a year. And Chisora's pre-fight weight of 18st 9lb (261 pounds) was the heaviest of his career and suggested that he'd taken a less-than-rigorous approach to his training.

It was Fury's jab that proved the most effective punch, with a short clubbing left also finding its target throughout.

Chisora rocked Fury in Round 2, and briefly had his man in trouble in the 3rd and 4th, but these were the only moments when he looked like he might do anything. From then on Fury cleared his head and dominated, throwing some beautiful combinations.

While Fury never looked like ending the fight early, Chisora cut an increasingly battered, bloodied, and disheartened figure as the fight wore on. At one stage his corner threatened to pull him out of the fight in an attempt to spark him into life. But it made little difference — he was worn down by Fury's constant physical dominance and relentless work rate. Despite a short flurry from Chisora in the 10th, he never looked like turning the fight around. He knew he needed a stoppage in the final round, but lacked any energy and intensity, as Fury managed to keep disappointing him at arm's length to take the fight by the judges' unanimous decision — along with the British and Commonwealth titles. 'This is a dream come true' said Fury, 'and it means the world to me.'

Round 3

Shadow Boxing

IN THE BUILD-UP TO THE FURY V CHISORA FIGHT, THE WBO, IBF, and WBA champion, Wladimir Klitschko, had openly discussed the prospect of facing the winner. Chisora had already seen two proposed bouts with Klitschko cancelled within the past eight months — and he still looked a long way short of a fighter ready to mix in such exulted company. Now the fifteenth victory of Fury's professional career opened the door to a possible world title shot against one of the two Klitschko brothers.

During the following year, Fury put away a further four heavyweights: Nicolai Firtha, Neven Pajkić, Martin Rogan, and Vinny Maddalone — all by TKO — all within five rounds. In a WBC world title eliminator on 1 December 2012, Fury won a unanimous decision over the American contender Kevin Johnson.

But during the week before the fight against Neven Pajkić, an interview with *The Guardian's* Donald McRae once again hinted at his inner troubles. Arriving at the Fury bungalow one morning, the fighter greets him. The journalist is amazed that Fury has such a soft handshake...

> There is no knuckle-crushing welcome from a Gypsy hard man ... The big man leads me round the back of the house he shares with his 21-year-old wife, Paris, and two children, Venezuela and Prince. The sight of the 2-year-old girl jumping around happily, and the 4-week-old baby boy sleeping in a pale blue pram, prompts a discussion of their exotic names.
>
> *One night, while I was sleeping, I thought of Venezuela. My wife is called Paris. I'm Tyson and* [gesturing to his son] *he's called Prince John James. If the girl had a normal name it wouldn't fit in, would it? I really wanted to call the boy Jesus but the wife didn't want it. I like that name. A lot of Mexicans are called Jesus.'*

Sitting in his armchair, wearing a vest and shorts, Fury began speaking about his upcoming Commonwealth title defence against the Bosnian-born Neven Pajkic, now Canada's heavyweight champion.

I went on TV in Canada and said exactly what I thought of Pajkić. I'd watched his fight and thought it was rubbish. From there it went really personal. He started calling me and my family names. I know this is terrible and I shouldn't say it, but I'm in the mode to do serious damage. When I go in there I'm trying to put my fist through the back of his head. I'm trying to break his ribs and make them stick out the other side. I don't like this kid. This kid has said some terrible things.

But gradually the conversation turned darker. The journalist, who had once interviewed Mike Tyson in his bleakest years, suddenly felt the same kind of chill when Fury began revealing his darker feelings.

There's a name for what I have, where one minute I'm happy, and the next minute I'm sad — like commit-suicide sad ...and for no reason – because nothing's changed. One minute I'm over the moon, and the next minute I feel like getting in my car and running it into a wall at a hundred miles an hour. I don't know what's wrong with me. I'm messed up. Can I overcome these feelings? No. I just live with them. I think I need a psychiatrist, because I do believe I am mentally disturbed in some way.

Maybe it was the fact that when I was a kid we didn't have a family life. My mother and father were always shouting and screaming and hitting each other. My dad had different women and different kids down the road. My mum had 14 pregnancies — but only four of us survived. We had a little sister born for a few days and she died. That would affect you.

I know I've got nothing to be upset about ... I'm British and Commonwealth champion, I'm doing OK.

I've got a few quid in the bank. I shouldn't be upset. But I don't feel I've done any good at all. I thought when the children were born it would be a top thing. And when I became English champion I thought there'd be a great feeling — but no. I thought it must be because it's not big enough. Let me win the British title. But after I took that off Chisora there was nothing. At the end of the day what have I done? I've beaten another man up in a fight. I dunno what I want out of life, me. What's the point of it all? ... Every day you're on a downward slope.

Depression runs in the family. My three brothers are the same as me. But with us everyone is a tough guy. But we all cry instantly. Look at me: 6ft 9, and if someone said this to me in my family I would just cry. All of us would. But nothing's talked about in our family. We just push other aside, or give each other a punch.

I don't think it's ever going to change. I can just see it going crazy. One loss in the ring and it's all over. So it's very serious. I know it could be all over every time I step into the ring.'

'I hear this constantly,' Paris Fury interrupts. 'But there are good days. If you'd come on a good day, you'd have been all right.'

'So, how would Fury cope if he woke up on Saturday in this depressed state of mind?' asked the interviewer.

> *I won't, I love boxing. It's not a horrible thing to me. I can't wait for the moment I step into the ring. I feel calm then. It's like everything has been forgotten. It's just me and him and we're going to go at it old school. But after that it's back to the reality and feeling angry – just with life. I'm looking for something different that's just not out there. But when I get in the ring I don't have this feeling I've got now. Right now, I really feel like smashing this place up. I don't feel like that in the ring because, if I do, it's all over. An upset fighter is a beaten fighter. I'm glad I've got boxing. I feel better in the ring. That's when I feel some relief.'*

But later that week, fighting Neven Pajkić, Tyson Fury hit the deck for the first time...

> *It was a right hand to the chin — a legitimate knockdown. But if you can open your eyes, you can get back up. And I thought 'Right, I'm going to kill you now. You've embarrassed me in front of all those*

people. I'm going to hurt you badly. I got straight back up and put him down three times.

Contradictions swirled around Fury — a man who could get back up and fight back from a smashing blow to the face, but who could be laid low by his own dark thoughts. It might've been possible to believe that Fury really did find his refuge in the ring. For a man who left school at the age of eleven, he could articulate the darkness within him in a startlingly matter-of-fact manner. There would be other times like this, deeper ...darker ...and longer.

Round 4

Furious

TYSON FURY MADE HIS US DEBUT AT MADISON SQUARE Garden, on 20 April 2013, when he fought the highly-ranked American, and former World Cruiserweight Champion, Steve Cunningham. As an IBF title eliminator, the winner would then fight the unbeaten Bulgarian, Kubrat Pulev, to earn a shot at the long-term world champion, the Ukrainian, Wladimir Klitschko.

Fury began the fight wildly and was floored in Round 2. But he soon regrouped and handed Cunningham the first KO of his career in Round 7. This victory now made the 24-year-old Fury number 7 in the BoxRec world rankings, the IBF number 2, the WBC number 6, and the WBO number 5.

In a sign of other controversies to come, before the fight, Fury told one interviewer that he would 'hang his own sister' if she was promiscuous. Later that year, in a bit of pre-match banter, he called out the fellow heavyweights he didn't think were in his class — and was fined £3,000 for suggesting that David Price and Tony Bellew were gay lovers.

* * *

Fury was due to meet David Haye on 28 September 2013, in his first ever pay-per-view contest. But the week before the fight Haye pulled out having sustained a cut above the eye during training which required six stitches. The fight was rescheduled for 8 February the following year. But in November, Haye now pulled out of the fight completely, citing a career-threatening shoulder injury that would require surgery. He went as far as hinting at retirement.

As a boxer, David Haye has sometimes given the impression of a man, almost literally, falling to pieces. On one occasion, he lost a fight due to a toe injury preventing him from getting leverage for his punches. During another fight, he snapped an Achilles tendon so that his foot flopped limply at the end of his leg like the limb of a rag doll.

But at the time, Fury was suggesting that Haye was making excuses because he didn't have the guts for the fight — or, as Barry McGuigan once said of the somewhat reluctant fighter Audley Harrison ...'due to problems with intestinal fortitude'.

> *I was absolutely furious, but in all honesty this was exactly what I expected. Everyone knows I was very suspicious when he pulled out the first time and this confirms to me that he'd always been afraid of me and never wanted the fight.*

Aside from all the logistics involved in setting up the training camp, Fury was most annoyed that Haye's shenanigans had cost him his positions in the world rankings — including the IBF final eliminator bout that would have led to a shot at the world title.

* * *

2014 wasn't a great year for Tyson Fury. In the February, the Furys were victims of an arson attack. Bombs were placed on the bonnets of cars in the driveway of his bungalow. One exploded, destroying his VW Passat. The other, on his BMW estate, failed to ignite. Luckily, the boxer and his family weren't at home, as he was training out of the country at a training camp.

There are some crazy people out there. It's upsetting to think that someone is going to your house and burning things down. It's just people being silly with jealousy and envy. They know I'm away so it is the perfect time to do it. Anybody could have been at home, it's a good job my wife and two kids were with me in France.

On the night of the actual fight he'd been training for, Fury duly dispatched the American, Joey Abell, in Round 4.

On 26 July, he was due to fight a rematch with Dereck Chisora, for both the European and British heavyweight titles — with the bout also being a WBO title eliminator. This time, the week before the fight, Chisora was forced to pull out after fracturing a hand during training. The Belarusian, Alexander Ustinov, was lined up as his replacement.

* * *

As Fury prepared to fight this new opponent, *Sportsmail* spent the day at his new training headquarters in Bolton. They reported that the man they met was a far cry from the one who had launched a foul-mouthed tirade at Chisora during a press conference the previous week. Maybe it was a bit of PR damage-limitation but, whatever the case, the Fury that

Sportsmail now encountered was polite, measured, and welcoming. But even at this early stage in his career, almost prophetically, he was beginning to contemplate a life without boxing...

> *I owe everything to boxing. I don't know what I'd do without it. I've got no education, I can hardly read, I can hardly write, my grammar's terrible, I can't spell. My skills are blagging, fighting, and hustling. I became a fighter because I had to. There was no other way of me becoming successful. I could've done what I needed to do to survive one day to the next but I wasn't going to settle for that. I wanted to be something different — and I'm still trying to be something different.*

As Tyson and his uncle and trainer, Peter Fury, prepared for a second workout of the day, two new faces appeared in the gym. Joe Holmen and girlfriend Sarah Kluetz had come from Norway to watch Fury train. They stayed for the gruelling hour-long session and left with a signed glove and plenty of memories. Sarah explained that the pair had spoken with Team Fury through social media and had asked to visit. 'He's different to other boxers, down to earth,' said Joe.

At times, that was true. But what was driving Fury was his desire to seal a place in boxing history. Perhaps that explains why, at other times, he gave the impression that he was rough and volatile.

> *History only remembers kings, not soldiers. There are plenty of people who have died in battle, and nobody remembers their names. I'd like to be remembered, but just being a world champion ain't going to cut it, because how many world champions have there been? There's hundreds of world titles - the WBU, the IBU, the WBF, the IBC, the ABC – but they don't mean anything. Mike Tyson is remembered for being the baddest man on the planet, not for being the youngest heavyweight champion of the world. It's bad things that get remembered – so I'm hoping to do a few bad things before I finish ... I couldn't give a flying fuck what no-one thinks — and if anybody thinks I overstepped the mark they can suck my balls.*

There were three training sessions a day, five times a week. Those, along with a strict diet, saw him hit his fighting weight – 18st 7lbs (259 pounds) – six weeks ahead of schedule. No mean feat considering he had weighed in at a career heavy 19st 8lbs (274 pounds) for his previous fight. There was also the temptation to avoid due to the fact that Fury's base was opposite a pastry shop, a pizza and kebab house, and a bakery. And a door further down was a pub and a fish 'n' chip shop.

> *There's no temptation because, whether people believe it or not, I'm a true athlete and I know what I have to do and how to do it. I'm a hundred per cent focused ... All my family believed from one amateur fight that I'd be heavyweight champion. We've had world champion bare-knuckle fighters, but I'd be the first person to win a world title in professional boxing. It'd be a special moment in our legacy.*

At this point many were openly speculating on what Tyson Fury might go on to achieve. Any number of things *could* happen. But there was probably only one reason why he might fail — and that would be Tyson Fury himself. Every fight he would go into would be his to lose. It remained to be seen whether Fury — a complicated man who knew nothing else but boxing, who didn't care what people thought, but who wanted to be remembered in history, who said that world titles were worthless, but knew what they meant to his family — could control himself and deliver.

Five months after the petrol bombing of the cars in his driveway, Tyson Fury's uncle, Hughie, suffered head injuries, a broken arm, and broken shinbone as the result of a bizarre accident while unhitching a caravan that then tumbled against him. After his leg was put in a cast, he left hospital without telling doctors, and without collecting anti-blood-clotting medication. On the afternoon of the 25 July, the day before the rescheduled fight, Peter Fury received a call saying his elder brother had undergone an operation to place a pin in his leg below the knee. The operation was a success as fully expected.

Unfortunately, a blood clot developed, as a consequence of having a cast on his leg, which had then travelled through to his arteries making the situation far worse. A week later, he went back into hospital to undergo emergency surgery. Hughie Fury was placed in an intensive care unit as everyone awaited news. He was said to be in a critical but stable condition.

It was Hughie Fury who had trained Tyson for his fights with John McDermott and Dereck Chisora. The situation was badly affecting Tyson, and a decision was taken to pull out rather than send him into the fight with his mind not focused. But when Fury received intense criticism for cancelling the fight, the family was forced to go public with the additional news that Paris had suffered a miscarriage five months into a pregnancy, with the fight scheduled to take place just days after the couple's loss.

Peter Fury revealed the situation: 'What people also don't know is that Tyson has had bad news of his wife having a miscarriage. As Tyson's trainer, I was not going into a contest with my brother in a hospital fighting for his life and his wife and children in despair.'

After eleven weeks in intensive care, Hughie Fury passed away. He never recovered from post-surgery complications.

The Fury v Chisora rematch eventually took place on 29 November 2014, in London. Once again, Fury dominated, using a southpaw stance for the majority of the fight. He won after his corner pulled Chisora out at the end of the Round 10.

This now meant that Fury was the WBO International, European, and British heavyweight champion.

Fury went on to face the European Champion, the Romanian-German, Christian Hammer, on 28 February 2015, at the O2 Arena in London, where he retained his WBO title. Right from the opening bell, Fury again dominated, dropping Hammer in Round 5 with a short right hook. The fight came to a halt in Round 8 when Hammer retired. After the fight, Fury began calling out Wladimir Klitschko, knowing he was now ready for a world-title shot.

Round 5

Fury v Klitschko

IN JULY 2015, THE WORLD HEAVYWEIGHT TITLE SHOWDOWN was announced when it was confirmed that Tyson Fury would fight Wladimir Klitschko for the unified WBA, IBF, WBO, IBO, Lineal, and *The Ring* heavyweight titles at the Esprit Arena in Düsseldorf, Germany. Initially scheduled for 24 October, the fight was postponed till 28 November after Klitschko sustained a calf injury. Meanwhile Fury began training with the two highest-ranked heavyweights in the world's premier kickboxing league (GLORY), Rico Verhoeven and Benjamin Adegbuyi.

* * *

In September 2015 — in the build-up to the fight — Fury said he wanted to run as an independent candidate, as MP for Morecambe and Lunesdale, saying that the government were too focused on immigrants and not enough on Britain's own homeless people. He also said that Britain should leave the EU. There were the predictable accusations of racism and xenophobia from the liberal left. When the Brexit referendum later made debate at least a little more possible when the majority of the British people agreed that immigration needed to be properly managed, before the country's public services and infrastructure — the National Health Service, schools, and social housing stock — buckled and collapsed under the sheer weight of numbers. So the views that Fury expressed at the time were subsequently shown to be squarely in the mainstream.

Appearing to be happier when creating controversy, once *that* reaction had died down, a few weeks later Fury now began arguing that performance-enhancing drugs (which he himself denied taking) should be permitted in boxing and other sports.

> *Why don't they just make drugs totally legal in sports, then everybody would be taking drugs, and then it would be fully fair then, wouldn't it? ... It's none of my concern really, but if the governing bodies want to do that then I think it would be a bit fairer because you've got all them people [sic] taking drugs and when you face a man who is not taking drugs it becomes unfair, doesn't it?*

When Lance Armstrong was finally nailed for winning 7 Tours de France through PEDs, he argued that he'd been forced to do it because everyone else was. And, truth be told, if the asterisks for 'drug cheating' against Armstrong's name in the record books were to be applied accurately across the board, where appropriate, the cycling record books for that era would begin to look a little threadbare. The trouble is, though, that if you allow drug use in order to level the playing field, then it's not the best athletes, cyclists, and boxers that win the prizes, but the best pharmacists.

* * *

In a pre-fight promo the week prior to the fight, Fury paced a boxing ring, mike in hand, as Klitschko looked up from a ringside seat...

> *And I know what 99.9% of you are thinking — you all expect me to lose to the great Wladimir Steelhammer. But I know, looking at him, that he's got a lot of doubt. He's thought deeply about this fight and he's very worried about it. And on Saturday night the whole world is gonna celebrate with me, because Tyson Fury will have achieved his goal to become the undisputed heavyweight champion of the world. I want you out of the heavyweight division [addressing*

Klitschko directly] because you have about as much charisma as my underpants.

Fury tells the story of how he had a 'sauna duel' with Klitschko which he considered gave him a psychological advantage going into the fight...

This was years before when I was about twenty-two. Everyone said that Klitschko was the Sauna King — everyone goes in to the sauna and has to stay in there longer – it's a mental thing he does to everybody. But everything's competition to me, one hundred per cent — basketball, PlayStation, I've got to win. I'm in there like a minute — I'm already totally fucked – gone. I'm thinking I can't do this, I really can't do it. We'd been sitting in the sauna for a long time – and it gets up to twenty minutes and he gets up and turns the heat up. I start counting up to ten, six times, for a minute, in my head. So I know it's a minute. If I pass out, I pass out. The boys 'll just bring me out and put some water on me and I'll be alright. Anyway, I put oil all over me, and I got this newspaper and I lay back reading this newspaper... And it gets to about forty-five minutes and he just gets up and walks out the door. Didn't even speak to anyone — just goes upstairs. And I thought I can't just get up and walk straight out, I had to leave it a few minutes. I'm nearly passing out and when I walked out the door. I was all lightheaded nearly gonna faint and someone said, 'What have you done to Klitschko?' I said, 'I've just won a mental battle with him.' I knew then I had him mentally. He knew he'd lost already. Great story. True story.

When the two sat face-to-face with him in a 'round table' mediated by Johnny Nelson before the fight – Fury brought the incident up but Klitschko claimed he didn't remember. Fury explained to the host...

I was at his training camp and there were about ten of us guys in the sauna. And one by one the other guys popped off and it came down to just Fury and Wladimir Klitschko in there ...[to Klitschko] *you remember?*

I remember the sauna, yes.

...and mentally, in my mind, I was still in a competition with him.

What are you talking about?

I was prepared to die in there before I'd have gone out. I was in there forty minutes. He got out first. I thought 'mental victory'.

But you're building your own world that didn't exist.

We both know it did exist.

I don't know what you're talking about.

You can say you don't know what I'm talking about...

I'm seriously saying it.

...but you know and I know ...you gave up.
No I don't.
...Yeah.

* * *

Before the fight, Fury claimed he'd been warned about potential cheating tactics by the Klitschko camp — although they never levelled any specific charge, nor provided any specific evidence. Fury refused to drink water that had been left in the locker room because of fears that it might have been spiked. But there were suspicions on both sides.

Just hours before the fight a row blew up over the thickness of the ring canvas. Fury complained to both the British Boxing Board of Control and the commissioner of the fight that there was too much foam under the canvas. The Fury camp believed it to be 5 inches thick, which made it a safety issue. It had been evident at Klitschko's training camp in Austria that his ring was particularly spongy, and that's was how he liked it, because it reduced his opponent's mobility while giving him extra purchase.

'They will have seen a lot of footage of Fury being incredibly mobile,' said the boxing pundit Steve Bunce, 'and of course his plan tonight will be to be very mobile and make Klitschko chase him. It might seem unfair, but it's the champion's prerogative. It'll prove a serious problem for Fury and nullify most of what he's prepared for.'

> *You can't learn it – you've either got it or you've not. Someone six-foot-nine shouldn't be able to move like I can. I defy every law of gravity. It really isn't fair that I move like I do — the reflexes, the slipping the sliding, the awkwardness — the ability to box both ways. I'm a naturally gifted talent.*

Eventually the ring underlay was torn up and the canvas was still being re-laid so close to fight time that there was a danger of the undercard being lost. Because of the last-minute canvas alterations Rod Stewart, who was set to perform before the fight, missed his sound check.

A further controversy blew up when, just minutes before the fight, Klitschko was accused of cheating — putting it on the verge of being called off. While the undercard played out in the ring an argument was raging between Peter Fury and Klitschko's trainer Bernd Bonte, after it transpired that the world champion had had his gloves wrapped without anyone in attendance to witness it from Fury's camp. The Klitschkos had insisted that Vitali watch Tyson's gloves being wrapped, and Team Fury assumed that this would be mutual — but Wladimir's gloves were on before they got to him.

Peter Fury threatened to call off the fight, storming away shouting, 'It's off, the fight's off!'

And there's no doubt whatsoever, that in front of fifty-five thousand people, in the Esprit Arena, there was a legitimate stand-off, and the entire Fury camp was most definitely prepared to walk out.

The entire schedule was delayed as Klitschko was forced to cut off the tape around his fists and have them rewrapped under the watchful eye of one of Fury's training team.

It all added further to the tension after Fury had been unable to get hold of his preferred gloves until the very morning of the fight. The Klitschko camp had wanted Fury to wear a certain brand of gloves that he wasn't used to wearing, which would come up bigger than he was used to. This was seen as further evidence of attempts to disturb his pre-fight preparation.

* * *

The question was posed: 'Who had the edge?' — the reigning WBA, IBF, and WBO champion of the world with twenty-six heavyweight title fights to his name; or the man who once beat Dereck Chisora? Klitschko had a good record against bigger fighters — 7-0 (with 6 KOs) against fighters taller than six-foot-six. A few others, Fury among them, would say that Klitschko was approaching forty, and on his way down. The bookies made Klitschko the 1/5 favourite, with Fury at 4/1. But Cassius Clay was a big underdog against Sonny Liston — and so was Leon Spinks against Muhammad Ali, and Buster Douglas against Mike Tyson. Underdogs won ...sometimes. Did anybody see it coming?

Although, next to the chiselled Klitschko, Fury still looked somewhat 'relaxed' around the waist, he was certainly fitter than he'd ever been – a stone (14 pounds) lighter than when he fought Christian Hammer in February. He was also the tallest man that Klitschko had ever faced, and one who had a four-inch reach advantage. But this wasn't Christian Hammer; this was 'Doctor Steelhammer'.

Social media was awash with speculation...

- How calm and classy is Klitschko?
- To my mind there is something more unsettling about his placid, controlled professionalism than any amount of grandstanding — the sinister nature of his almost unapproachable focus.
- Well, err... good luck then, Tyson Fury.
- I don't think he will be able to get himself through more than half a fight before running out of gas, after which Klitschko will start to turn the screw.

* * *

Tyson Fury makes his way to the ring — it's a fairly low-key entrance. He's wearing a T-shirt with a picture of his late uncle Hughie printed on it. There are a few token 'boos' from the crowd. The music that Fury has chosen for his ring walk is Randy Travis' *I'm Gonna Have A Little Talk (With Jesus)*.

Then Klitschko appears — accompanied by that traditional Ukrainian folk band, the Red Hot Chilli Peppers. Fury shadow boxes as he waits for his opponent to step in to the ring. He looks calm, bored even — like a man waiting for another win to turn up, as if it might be a train running a bit late — or as if he's trying to remember if he watered the plants before he left home. Fury talks to his opponent all the way through the preamble.

Round 1: It's a slow opening round, with Klitschko unable to connect with his famous jab, as Fury 'twitches' this way and that. In the first ninety seconds, neither man lands a clean blow or a decent punch — until Fury gets in the first proper shot with a straight jab to the face. Fury throws a few more punches and scores with the one power punch of the round.

Fury's round.

Round 2: Fury again lands the first blow of any note. Then Klitschko lands a jab to the head and then the body, as he suddenly realizes he has to get involved. He's trying to be more aggressive than in the opening round, moving forward, working off his jab, but yet to risk throwing a right hand. Fury steps up and rattles Klitschko with a combination to the head.

Round 2 to Fury.

Round 3: Fury is showing that he can stay with the champ. And the longer he stays — and stays ahead — the more his confidence is building. His hands are already hanging low — hardly a sign of feeling intimidated. Suddenly Fury switches to southpaw, completely disrupting Klitschko's building rhythm. Fury is tempting the champ to come forward, but he doesn't bite. Only three punches are landed in the entire round, two of them by Fury. So far in the fight, Fury has landed seventeen punches to Klitschko's eleven.

It's closer, but it's another round to Fury.

Round 4: Klitschko is leaning in now. Fury seems almost bored but then unleashes a hook that Klitschko manages to fend off. Klitschko gets in his first good right of the fight, just as the bell sounds — the first time Fury has looked remotely troubled. Klitschko's corner tell him to start throwing more of these power shots.

Klitschko's round.

Round 5: Klitschko is cut underneath the eye, the first physical sign of damage. [The replays show the cut was caused by a clash of heads rather than a blow.] Fury takes a swing, so wild that he turns himself around in the opposite direction, before he dances away. As the round ends, Klitschko misses a right over the top. One hopeful commentator thinks Klitschko is luring Fury into a sense of overconfidence he can take advantage of.

Fury's round.

Round 6: Fury gets in two good jabs, but Klitschko doesn't reply and comes in to clinch. Klitschko just isn't throwing punches. Fury has now thrown 162 punches to Klitschko's 96. 'Watch out,' say Fury's corner, 'he'll take a chance soon.'

Round to Fury.

Round 7: Fury again switches stances and makes it tough for the champ to settle. Now he comes forward and Klitschko has to duck under a sharp right hook. Fury lands one good jab to Klitschko's face and a few glancing rights. Klitschko waits …and waits …and waits. It's already getting to the point where he'll need a KO to win.

Fury's round

Round 8: Fury hardly has to do anything more than control Klitschko, whose unwillingness or inability, to fight is now plain for all to see. Then, for the first time in the fight, Klitschko rallies slightly and gets his jab working, landing two good blows on his opponent.

Klitschko's round.

Round 9: The champ is definitely trying to wake up now, but a big left hook from Fury throws Klitschko off balance, and another cut opens up on the Ukranian's forehead. A nice right hand from Klitschko jars Fury. Fury gets a warning for a rabbit punch.

Another round to Klitschko.

Round 10: Fury realized *he* now has to do more and comes in, working Klitschko with a few jabs to the body. Klitschko brushes Fury with a jab and the challenger returns fire with more glancing body blows. The pair barge into each other as they walk to their corners.

Fury takes the round.

Round 11: By now Klitschko needs a knockout. But will home advantage tell with the judges? He doesn't look at all urgent in the ring. Another cut opens on Klitschko's face, although it could have been a further clash of heads. Klitschko goes for a big left, misses, and Fury connects. Fury is docked a point for another rabbit punch, even though Klitschko had his back turned, neglecting to 'defend himself at all times'.

Klitschko's round by 2 points.

Round 12: At last, there's a big right from Klitschko, who has to go for the knockout now. It rocks Fury but he stays up, and that's all he needs to do now. Klitschko comes forward and lands another good shot. Is it too little, too late? The bell goes and Fury celebrates like he's won the fight. But what will the judges say?

The fight stats tell the story...

Punches thrown: Klitschko: 69 / Fury: 202.
Punches landed: Klitschko: 52 / Fury: 86.
Power blows: Klitschko: 18 / Fury: 48.

The judges' cards are collected and the announcement made. There is to be no controversy. Fury has won by a unanimous points' decision: 116–111, 115–112, 115–112.

Fury thanks Jesus and breaks down in tears. '...*My rock, my salvation. I can't believe it. It's hard to come to a foreign*

country and win. When I got the point docked I thought I'd lost.'

He apologises for the antics in the build-up in the fight, saying he was just trying to show he was younger and more hungry. He serenades his wife with some Aerosmith — as some wit points out that this might be worse than the punishment he'd dished out to Klitschko.

* * *

Just twenty-four hours before the fight, Paris Fury had broken down in tears while telling her husband she was again pregnant. It was an emotional moment for the pair, after the trauma of the miscarriage the year before. She believed the news they were going to have another child is what inspired him to victory.

Tyson himself believed that the most significant inspiration came from the unusual appearance of a bee that buzzed around his head during the middle rounds of the fight — convinced that this was a sign that his uncle Hughie's spirit was with him, helping him.

John Fury had his own reasons for believing that his son would prevail. While sitting in his hotel room before the fight, thinking and praying about it, the entire room had filled with light.

* * *

It was often a messy fight but Fury won by virtue of his superior boxing skills, mobility, and head movement — as well as his ability to switch between orthodox and southpaw. Klitschko could neither work out, nor outwork, the challenger — who fully deserved to be awarded the unanimous decision. Fury had now become only the fifth British *bona fide* world heavyweight champion, following Bob Fitzsimmons, Lennox Lewis, Frank Bruno, and David Haye.

As the result of winning a truckload of titles, and a reputed £4m in prizemoney, Tyson Fury was rocketed to instant stardom. While Paris Fury feared that his new celebrity status might stop them from enjoying a normal life, she doubted it would change him as a person.

> I don't think fame will change Tyson, or us, or change the way we feel or what we do. Things will change because we ain't gonna be able to go nowhere, no more. Just walking round a shopping centre won't be an option. You get the odd fool. If Tyson was short-

tempered it might cause problems, but thankfully he's not. He's never had a fight outside the ring ever.

With her last comment, maybe Paris Fury was recalling what had happened with Tyson's father, John, a few years earlier, when he'd got into a fight against three other men at a car auction in Manchester.

> *One feller bit my dad on the face and, as he shoved him back, he punched the feller in the eye. He lost the eye when he had to have it taken out because it got infected. The judge found my dad guilty of wounding with intent. I've never been in trouble in my life. I've not got a criminal record. ...Never had a fight outside boxing. So I'm very different to my dad.*

John Fury was jailed for gouging the eye of a former friend over a 12-year feud triggered by a row about a bottle of beer. He declared himself the toughest man in Britain before plunging his fingers into Oathie Sykes' eye socket, leaving him half blind. John Fury begged Manchester Crown Court for leniency, saying, 'I'm worried about my son. His boxing career is on the line.' John Fury got eleven years but was released early and managed to get special permission to leave the country to watch his son's title fight in Dusseldorf.

* * *

Tyson Fury was put on the shortlist for the *2015 BBC Sports Personality of the Year*. But the nomination generated a lot criticism, and stirred up a lingering controversy started by comments he'd made before the Klitschko fight.

> *There are only three things that need to be accomplished before the devil comes home. One of them is homosexuality being legal, one is abortion, and the other is paedophilia. Who would've thought, in the 50s and early 60s, that the first two would be legalised. People can say, 'Oh, you're against homosexuality, you're against abortions, you're against whatever.' But my faith and my culture are all based on the Bible. The Bible was written a long time ago, wasn't it, from the beginning of time until now? So if I follow that and that tells me it's wrong, then it's wrong for me.*

Almost 140,000 people signed an online petition saying that his views on made him an unsuitable candidate for the award.

'Tyson Fury cannot be a dickhead *and* win Sports Personality of the Year,' said the BBC's Clive Myrie.

'Hopefully I don't win SPOTY as I'm not the best role model in the world. Give it to someone who would appreciate it.' Fury tweeted shortly after the petition against his participation had been launched.

Asked directly if he was homophobic, Fury replied, *'No, definitely not. I wouldn't be a very good Christian if I hated anybody. If Jesus loves the world, I love the world.'*

But it was hardly the best way to answer the charge that he was homophobic by saying that his critics could suck his balls — or calling those who signed the petition '50,000 wankers'.

Neither did it help adding that the Olympic and World champion heptathlete, Jessica Ennis-Hill (also a contender for the BBC award) 'slaps up good.' [Though, in context, he simply meant that she looked good in 'slap' — i.e. 'make-up' — and not 'slapped', as in 'being hit'.]

On 8 December 2015, the SNP's John Nicolson — a member of the Culture, Media, and Sport Committee — challenged the BBC over Fury's nomination.

A mere ten days after he'd won his world heavyweight IBF title, Fury was stripped of it when it became known that he'd signed a separate agreement with Klitschko for a rematch, meaning he couldn't face the association's mandatory challenger Vyacheslav Glazkov.

In a further move, the Sports Journalists' Association withdrew an invitation to Fury to attend the British Sports Awards in London.

Greater Manchester Police then confirmed that they were investigating an alleged hate crime by Fury in relation to comments about homosexuality on Victoria Derbyshire's BBC TV programme — but they quickly backtracked, saying that no 'crime' had actually been committed, only what they called 'a hate incident' had occurred, so no charge would be laid.

On the same day, in what was beginning to look very much like a coordinated effort, The British Boxing Board of Control met and agreed to summon Fury to explain his recent comments.

Meanwhile, BBC bosses were fighting a frantic battle to save their award show after another contender, the long jumper Greg Rutherford, somewhat hypocritically, threatened to pull out. This would be the same 'bastion of morality', Greg Rutherford, who in his autobiography *The Unexpected* lifted the lid on the bedroom-hopping antics he'd enjoyed at one of his first athletics championships.

> I was exposed to — and involved in — the hedonistic and promiscuous behaviour that is a familiar theme at the end of major championships. Sometimes I found myself — and more than one other couple — going at it in the same room. On the night of the closing ceremony

there was a big party, and I found what went on absolutely unreal. I was staggered by just how many people got absolutely smashed and the bedroom-hopping that took place left, right and centre ...It was my first experience of the pulling power of the accreditation we all wore around our necks. As I subsequently learned, the older members of our team referred to it as a 'pussy pass' because, well, it unlocked a few doors ...English athletes were heavily criticised for not winning enough medals and I could see why — some of them seemed more intent on having fun and being a bit naughty than trying to set personal bests. I'm not sure the culture has changed that much since.

Perhaps Tyson Fury's comments about promiscuity had stirred a deeper discomfort in Rutherford than first met the eye.

Fury was in his car when he was stopped by a BBC reporter. The interview aired on national news, as a promotional boost for the show. Fury's answer came before the first question was even completed...
Tyson, have you got anything you can tell us about —
I've got lots that I can tell you.
Is that your reaction to the people who want you off the SPOTY shortlist?

Believe in the Lord, Jesus Christ, and you will be saved.

And what about being stripped of your belt — you must be very unhappy with that?

Jesus loves me — and he loves you, too.

And do you think you'll win SPOTY? Do you want to win SPOTY?

John 3:16 — God so loved the world that he sent his only begotten son. Whoever believes in him shall have eternal life and shall not perish. [Fury had worn 3:16 emblazoned on his shorts when he fought Chisora.]

Er... any final message for those who've criticized you — the people signing petitions, the Scottish independent... all sorts of people...? Just give us your take on it. Do you stand by your comments?

Believe in —

OK Tyson, thanks for stopping.

The awards show went ahead as planned. Tyson Fury finished in fourth; with 'Saint' Greg Rutherford finishing ninth in the public vote. At the ceremony, Fury apologised for his comments.

* * *

On 15 December, 2015, an article appeared in the Australian version of the *Sun* newspaper in which 25-year-old Baillie Mansell claimed she'd had an affair with Fury after they'd met in a bar in Manchester, in the September, after he'd secretly split from his wife back when he was training to fight Dereck Chisora. At pains to prove that she wasn't fantasizing, she described Fury's 'really flowery bedding, with poppies on it'. Paris Fury hinted at marital difficulties, with a tweet reading, 'I've found the key to happiness. Stay the hell away from arseholes.'

But the affair was already beginning to fizzle out as Fury prepared to fight Chisora. Baillie Mansell said, 'I always knew we weren't going to be a long-term thing. He made it clear he wanted to try to make it work with Paris but he didn't know if he could. Then he'd say it was never going to work and it was over with her. He changed his tune a lot.'

Paris Fury called Ms Mansell. 'I know we were separated, but before I move on I want some truths. No arguments with you, just some things I need to know. We went through a rough patch but we want to make it work. You must understand that. You seem a really nice girl and I'm sorry if you've got caught up in the middle of something'. The two spoke for nearly an hour.

Not long after, Fury tweeted: 'Big thanku & much respect to my darling wife @parisfury1, the apple of my eye. Not easy being married to jack the lad 6 years. Sorry!'

When the *Sun* contacted Fury for a comment, he replied in typically forthright manner. 'I have no idea what you are on about, sir, and I couldn't give a fuck what you print, you prick. Now suck my balls you fucking idiot. Now you've been told. Now fuck off.'

His lawyers said that it was a private matter.

* * *

After several months of negotiations, the rematch with Klitschko was finally announced on 8 April 2016 — with the fight scheduled to take place on 9 July, on Fury's home turf at the Manchester Arena.

In May, the Fury team released a training camp video which included Fury expressing his opposition to transgenderism, and bestiality becoming accepted. There was the predictable reaction, including complaints to the British Boxing Board of Control, with calls for Fury to be barred from his sport for offensive and racist remarks. Fury again apologised.

> *I would like to put on record that I am not homo-*
> *phobic. I have homosexual friends and I do not judge*
> *them because of their sexuality. My comments that*
> *you may have read are from the Holy Scriptures, and*
> *this is what I live from.*

Apparently one of Tyson's uncles was gay and, according to his father, Tyson got on as well with him as he did any other member of the family.

> *I apologise to anyone who may have taken offence at any of my comments. I said some things, which may have hurt some people, which as a Christian man is not something I would ever want to do. Though it is not an excuse, sometimes the heightened media scrutiny has caused me to act out in public. I mean no harm or disrespect to anyone and I know more is expected of me as an ambassador of British boxing and I promise in future to hold myself up to the highest possible standard. Anyone who knows me personally knows that I am in no way a racist or bigot, and I hope the public accept my apology.*

It was another of Fury's uncles, Ernest, a born-again Christian and preacher, who'd strongly influenced the young Tyson's beliefs. In the home where Tyson Fury grew up, a Bible was always open on a stand. It was mainly from Uncle Ernest's interpretations of the Bible that Fury's more-fundamental beliefs seemed to spring. He took 'the Word', at its word.

'*I believe that all is revealed to us when we die,*' Fury once said. Unlike most boxers, he has never had tattoos done, as the book of Leviticus counsels against them. He was as bewildered as many people were — perhaps even the majority of other people — by the explosion of ideologies we were now suddenly required to embrace without question.

Gender equality and inclusion might be one thing. But, in the name of progressiveness and liberalism, the aspirations of many clamouring minorities had become increasingly loud, bizarre, and unreal. And there were far more-extreme and deadly beliefs than Tyson Fury's now doing the rounds — like believing that there are forty virgins waiting for you in paradise if you blow up a tube train full of passengers with a rucksack full of dynamite.

Despite all this bluster and controversy, it has to be realized that it would be simply impossible to have become a world heavyweight champion without supreme levels of discipline, competitive intelligence, and tactical wit. Yes, either side of his stunning world title victory, Fury had spoken contentiously. But in the midst of it all, he had fought a brilliantly controlled bout to take the title. It was a staggering achievement for a man who, five years earlier, had been living in a caravan in Morecambe — but whose life had now taken on a peculiar blend of the disciplined, the disorderly, and the doctrinal.

Round 6

Gathering Moss

O N 24 JUNE, THE FURY-KLITSCHKO REMATCH WAS AGAIN postponed, after Tyson Fury sustained a sprained ankle in training. On the same day, he and his cousin, Hughie, were charged by UK Anti-Doping, having tested positive for the banned substance nandrolone, discovered in a sample taken back in February 2015. The two strenuously denied the charge. On 23 September, Fury again postponed the fight after being declared medically unfit. It was reported by *ESPN* that he'd failed another drug test the previous day.

Press conferences were scheduled ...and postponed. Just prior to one, Fury claimed he couldn't make it because his car had broken down. At another one that he *did* manage to attend, he arrived with five cheerleaders in tow — a variation on the year before, when he'd showed up in a full Batman costume, accompanied by his cousin Hughie, in a bright-yellow Lamborghini Aventador.

When he was eventually questioned, the accusation was levelled that he'd been putting off the rematch because he was scared of losing his title.

> *How can I be scared? I'm 28-years-old. I believe I'm the greatest out of everyone that's ever lived. Klitschko got played with the first time. He didn't even win a round. He lost every round — he couldn't even land a punch. Why would I need to be scared of him, a 40-year-old man?*

'So, did you push back your rematch with Klitshcko because you were suffering from depression and you weren't training?' *'...To be honest... yes.'*

If Tyson Fury is one thing, he is honest, sometimes searingly so — about his mood swings, his attitudes to women, his heritage, his public persona, his religious beliefs. His relationship with his Twitter account is like others have with a psychotherapist. You can ask him pretty much anything and he'll furnish you with a reply.

The anticipation of a desired outcome is often more satisfying than the outcome itself — as we adapt to it and the excitement gradually fades. In Tyson Fury's case it happened almost instantaneously...

> *I expected more than actually there was. I was expecting ... 'more'. If I had a hundred million in the bank, I'd expect to feel different. If I bought a Ferrari or a Bentley, whatever — it didn't mean anything.*

There was no substance to it. Nothing had value. Nothing. Even being lineal champion of the world, and all those belts, and beating the great man undefeated in eleven years. It didn't have any meaning to it ...or value. It wasn't an achievement for me. Seven billion people in the world, and I was the man who became world heavyweight champion. But it didn't mean anything. It didn't mean as much as these slippers on my feet.

When you've done all that, what's it about then? These belts are worthless pieces of shit. When you've won all the world title belts, there's nothing left after that except defending them — like Klitschko did for fourteen years ... I didn't want to go down the route of fighting forty-odd nobodies. I was either going to be the best or I wasn't. And if I wasn't, then go ahead and beat me up. Anyone can beat Tyson Fury — all you've got to do is knock me out.

After his stunning upset victory over Klitschko, the previous year, Tyson Fury now engaged in one of the greatest acts of self-sabotage in the history of sport. That May, he'd abandoned his training camp in Holland, beginning a downward spiral that culminated with the news about cocaine use. In October, Fury admitted he'd spent the past few months snorting cocaine, drinking daily, and getting 'fat as a pig' to help deal with both the abuse he got, along with the onset of an episode of suicidal depression. So was he clean when he was actually fighting, with no drugs in his system?

No drugs at all, no drugs at all. I have never ever taken a drug to help me box in my life. Never took a performance-enhancing drug ever. Never even took an aspirin for a cold. I'm a natural. The only person that can beat me is me.

It's got nothing to do with my fighting — nothing to do with anything like that. What I'm going through at the moment is my personal life. I've not been in the gym since May. I went over to Holland to do a training camp and was crying every night. I didn't want to be there. I said to Peter, 'I can't do this anymore. I'm breaking down. There's something wrong with me. I don't want it. I wanna go home. Take everything and chuck it in the bin, I don't want it no more.'

From that day forward, I've never done any training. I've been out drinking Monday to Friday to Sunday. The only thing that helps me is when I get drunk out of me mind, and that's it. I don't tell lies. I've no need to tell lies. I've taken drugs, cocaine, on many occasions for the last six months. Not to enhance my performance – cos I've not even been performing.

[When taken outside of competition, cocaine isn't always a banned substance — it's considered a recreational drug rather than a performance-enhancing one. The British Boxing Board of Control has no clear rules about it, and abides by UK Anti-Doping Agency rules. For their part UKAD adheres to the World Anti-Doping Authority (WADA), which doesn't ban cocaine use outside of competition. The belt sanctioning bodies, the WBA and WBO, also follow WADA.]

They tested me about six times within a few weeks. Only recently, three days ago, last week, they came to my house at 1-30 in the morning, tested me, and came back at 9 am to test me again. What is this? Do you understand the treatment I'm getting off these people? They're driving me mad.

It's crazy what's going on but I don't really care. They've won. They've got what they wanted. That's it. I'm as fat as pig. I'm 285 pounds, 290 pounds. It is what it is. I've been an emotional wreck. I've been out trying to handle me life.

* * *

On October 4, *Rolling Stone* published a rambling and painful interview which laid bare the darkness that Tyson Fury had become swallowed up in. The interviewer felt obliged to include some background for US readers not familiar with Fury's muscular, patriarchal world of blood ties and blood feuds, where women have few rights.

> Fury is an Irish traveller, one of 40,000 nomadic people who live throughout Ireland and the UK in tight-knit caravan communities, working on construction, maintaining devout religious beliefs, and fighting among themselves for sport ...[but] often representing, in the public mind, a shiftless, criminally-inclined people who refuse to settle into jobs. Many RV parks in the UK have signs stating: 'No music after 11 PM. No travellers. All dogs must be kept on leads.' Fury is a ferocious and spectacular boxer who has risen higher than any traveller fighter in history, yet he claims his prestige has done little to change his treatment.

> *You know, I've been fighting them for a lot of years. Now, I just don't know. I just can't see a light at the end of the tunnel. ...If I'm honest. It's driving my family apart. My wife says she can't live with me because I'm a lunatic ... I'll lose my family, my wife, my kids — everything. All due to boxing. I wish to God*

that I'd never got into boxing as a child. I wish this had never happened and I had just done a routine job and a routine life. This is how it's got me. It's shoved wedges between my team, my uncles, cousins, relatives — everybody who's involved in boxing. Everyone is unhappy and it's all because of me. I feel like I'm the one who's brought all the pressure on everybody. I'm the one who's done all this. It's my burden to carry. Why should everybody else have to carry it around with them, just because they trained me?

Yeah, I've done cocaine. Plenty of people have done cocaine. What the fuck has that got to do with anything? It ain't a performance-enhancing drug. Am I not allowed to have a life now as well? Do they want to take my personal life off me too? I've not been in a gym for months. I've not been training. I've been going through depression. I just don't want to live anymore, if you know what I'm saying. I've had enough of it. They've forced me to the breaking edge. Never mind cocaine. I just don't care. I don't want to live anymore. So cocaine is a little minor thing compared to not wanting to live anymore.
I never took other drugs, ever, in me life. I only started to take cocaine in the last few months. I was a lot happier when I wasn't the world champion,

because people weren't giving me as much shit. I've been pushed to the brink. I can't take no more. I'm in a hospital at the moment. I'm seeing psychiatrists. They say I've got a version of bipolar. I'm a manic depressive. All from what they've done to me. All this shit through boxing, through taking titles, through writing me off. I beat the best man but I'm still shit.

From then on, it's been nothing more than a witch hunt. From then on, they've tried to get me chucked out of boxing because they can't tame me, they can't hire me. But I'm not for sale, no one can turn a key in my back, no one can do nothing to stop me. So now they're saying I took some cocaine and whatever. Listen if I had some smack I'd take it. If I had heroin I'd take that, never mind cocaine, for what they've done to me. It's a travesty what they've done. I want to expose them for what they are. The British Boxing Board of Control is in on it too. They're all in it together. The drug-testing companies are in on it as well. If I tested positive in February for drugs [several months before his match with Klitschko] *why let me fight the long-reigning champion and leave* [sic] *him of all his belts in November? Why not strip me in February.*

I get no credit for defeating the second-longest reigning champion in history. Even my own country where I was born and raised hates me. The only thing the Press wants to write is negativity. As soon as I won the title I got back off the boat and picked up the newspaper. It wasn't: 'He's dethroned the best man who's been in a long time.' It was that he's done this and he's done that — anything to try and take credit away from me.

It's been a witch hunt ever since I won that world title, because of my background, because of who I am and what I do – there's hatred for travellers and gypsies around the world ... If I won over 30 fights and knocked out everybody it would be no good he says I can't do nothing in my life that's any good to the general people because I'll never be accepted for who I am and what I am ...I'm the heavyweight champion of the world and I've been told 'Sorry mate you can't come in. No travellers allowed.'

People have got to understand that our lifestyle is totally, totally different. We may be the same colour, and we may speak the same language, but deep inside we are nothing alike. We are aliens.

Fury's inevitable tweets — which ranged from profane rants and impromptu rap videos, to a Photoshopped image of himself sitting behind a mountain of cocaine — were once followed by an announcement of his retirement, then an immediate retraction: *'Ha ha ha ha, u think you will get rid of the GYPSYKING that easy!!! I'm here to stay.'*

Just after Tyson became world champion, John Fury says that, as he jogged along the road in his Team Fury tracksuit, he was often jeered at by passers-by, driving with their windows down and shouting 'Pikey'.

As the most high-profile traveller in the world, Fury was baited relentlessly with responses to his tweets.

Make up your mind, ya fat pikey.'

[The term 'pikey' has a long history and was first defined as 'a person of the turnpike: the place where itinerant travellers and thieves would camp near a settlement.']

Some insulted him using the Irish jibe 'knacker'.

Others stuck to 'gypsy cunt'.

That same year, the world champion, his wife, and their three children were refused service in a restaurant due to their heritage. His rants and his dramatics, said Fury, were desperate backlashes — his way of hitting back at a culture that had discriminated against him his entire life – and which had now gone into overdrive since his title victory. Fury believed that the British press was hounding him just as much as social media, and that he was also receiving unfair scrutiny from boxing authorities. It all gave the impression that, rather than being a kindred spirt of his namesake Mike Tyson, Fury had more in common with the Jack Johnson — the world's first black heavyweight champion, who people would stop at nothing to try and unseat.

> *I feel more racism now in 2016 than any slave — any foreign immigrant ever did in the 1800s. When Muhammad Ali threw his gold medal away in the 1960s for being mistreated and abused, this is what I'm doing today. I'm throwing all my world titles in the bin because I ain't accepted in society for being a traveller in 2016. What does it mean to be a world heavyweight champion when you cannot go into your local restaurant, sit down and have a dinner? Clearly, it doesn't mean a thing.*
>
> *You don't have to take my word for it. Just go on my Twitter page and have a look. Scroll down for the last few months. Go online and read the articles by so-called British journalists. Read what they've got to say. No one can say a good thing. Whatever I do… If I won 30 fights and knocked out everybody, it would be no good. If it was the best maths teacher in the world, I would be no good. If I was the United States president, I'd be no good. I can do nothing in my life*

that's any good to people because I'll never be accepted for who I am and what I am. You could go and ask a hundred people about travellers and they've all got nothing good to say about them. I don't know where it comes from. I do not know where it comes from.

I am a gypsy and that's it. I will always be a gypsy, I'll never change. I will always be fat and white and that's it. I am the champion, yet I am thought of as a bum. I am moving out of the country. I am going to America where champions are better thought of. I am moving to Los Angeles where people have a better life. I made the decision last week to go where people admire success.

Why would I want to entertain people who hate me? I'm not gonna go in there and risk brain damage every time I go into a fight for people that don't give me no credit. All the money in the world ain't worth it to be trapped how I got trapped.

I used to love boxing when I was a kid. It was my life. All the way through it was my life. You finally get to where you need to be and it becomes a big mess. And that's it. I hate boxing now. I wouldn't even go across the road to watch a world title fight. That's what it's done to me.

I don't see a way out. I don't even see a way of living for me. I don't want to live anymore. It has brought me to the brink of, of death. It all seems so sad but it is the truth and I really don't care about boxing or sports or anything about it. I'm just sad that I got involved in boxing in the beginning. 'Cause I always thought once I get to the top, it will all change, but I knew deep down inside it would never change.

Tyson Fury had fulfilled the destiny his father had seen for him — even as a tiny baby that nearly died three times — and become the undisputed heavyweight champion of the world. But instead of being led to the celestial city on the hill, he'd been led into the dark night of his soul.

I don't even want to wake up. I hope I die every day. And that's a bad thing to say when I've got three children and a lovely wife isn't it? But I don't want to live anymore. And if I could take me own life – and I wasn't a Christian – I'd take it in a second. I just hope someone kills me before I kill me self. I'll have to spend eternity in hell.

I'm in a very bad place at the moment. I don't know whether I'm coming or going. I don't know what's going to happen to me. I don't know if I'm going to see the year out to be honest. I am seeking help, but they can't do nothing for me. What I've got is incurable. I don't want to live. All the money in the world, fame, glory — means nothing if you're not happy.

Fearing that it was only a matter of time before he was stripped of his belts, on 12 October, 2016, Tyson Fury relinquished his titles — to remove himself from continual pressure, give himself time to recover, and spend time with his family. Hours later, the British Boxing Board of Control said Fury had been 'temporarily relieved of his license pending further investigation into anti-doping and medical issues'.

Typically, Fury made no attempt to disguise his emotions.

I now enter another big challenge in my life which I know, like [my fight] against Klitschko, I will conquer …It is for the good of boxing and only fair and right to give up my belts …I won the titles in the ring and I believe that they should be lost in the ring, but I'm unable to defend at this time and I have taken the hard and emotional decision to now officially vacate my treasured world titles.

In his own statement, Fury's promoter Mick Hennessy said this 'heart-breaking' decision would allow him the 'time and space to recover from his present condition without any further pressure and with the expert medical attention he requires.'

BBC Radio 5's live boxing correspondent, Mike Costello, commented: 'First of all, Tyson Fury needs to get himself medically fit, then it's up to him and his uncle and trainer Peter Fury, and promoter Mick Hennessy, to decide what route they want to take. Will he be fit enough and able enough to go straight back in for a world title shot or will he need a warm-up contest before he fights again? It's so unclear at this stage because of the medical situation.'

* * *

As the weeks and months passed, with neither an indefinite ban nor a date set for a return, Tyson Fury now found himself in a state of limbo. He tweeted his frustration.

How long must I be held up and kept out of action? It's been 15 months since I've been under investigation. You're keeping an innocent man from filling [sic] *his destiny and from providing for his*

family. Everybody else is dealt with in a few months. Why must I be treated differently? Surely there must be a Human Rights law from preventing this from happening to people! Either ban me or set me free! I want to move on with my life. Clear my name and let me return to my former glory.
#innocentmansetmefree

Fury's close friend, the WBO middleweight champion Billy Joe Saunders, said, 'It is a big mistake, taking his boxing licence away. It's like taking food from a baby. He needs the licence to pull through.'

'It's driven him to despair,' said Peter Fury, who added hopefully, 'but I see him being back in the gym in March or April. He'll return stronger and reclaim what's rightfully his.'

During Tyson Fury's hiatus, the former Olympic champion, Anthony Joshua, had now risen to pre-eminence in the heavyweight division. But even as Fury's greatest rival and potential opponent, Joshua showed some sympathy and understanding. 'Tyson is a fighting man, a real talent, and he's good for boxing …in his own way. It's too easy to point the finger, because none of us really knows what he's going through.'

* * *

Tyson Fury had reached the pinnacle of boxing and shocked the world by beating the long-reigning champion. He was having an almighty struggle with having achieved his lifelong ambition with nothing now to replace it.

> *You have a goal in mind from being a child - and you achieve it... When I was an amateur I used to watch Wladimir Klitschko on TV and he was my target. When I beat him: that was my Everest. I tried retiring, but it wasn't enough. I tried golfing, clay pigeon shooting, 4x4-ing, strip clubs... but I had an emptiness inside.*

> *I hit the drink, I hit the drugs and I was out all night with hookers. I'd never taken a drug until I was 27; cocaine was the usual one, cocaine and alcohol. I look back on it now and I think, 'Would I change that?' But I wouldn't, I wouldn't change a thing because I knew it had to happen.*

> *I'd wake up and think, 'Why did I wake up this morning?' And this is coming from a man who had everything — money, fame, glory, titles, a wife, family and kids — everything. I just wanted to die, and I wanted to have fun doing it. But when the drink wears off it just leaves you with a bad hangover and even worse depression. But I felt as if I had nothing, a*

gaping hole that was just filled with gloom and doom. I was waking up and didn't want to be alive I was making everyone's life a misery; no-one could talk any sense into me at all.

In his darkest of all moments, he came seconds away from hurtling himself into a bridge in the new Ferrari convertible he'd just bought.

I was in it on the highway and I got the car up to 190mph and heading towards a bridge. I didn't care about nothing. I just wanted to die so bad. I gave up on life, but as I was heading to the bridge I heard a voice saying, 'No, don't do this Tyson, think about your kids, your family, your sons and daughter growing up without a dad.' I pulled off the motorway, I didn't know what to do, I was shaking, I was so afraid. I said I'd never think about taking my own life again.

A psychiatrist labelled Fury 'an imminent death risk', and his father had to take him in to the family home for safety reasons as his mental health began to deteriorate. In the house that John Fury had built in Styal, he watched over Tyson as he slept. In a darkly comic note: John had built the house with the ceilings high enough for him to stand up in but not anticipating that his sons, especially Tyson, would grow so tall, and have to walk around with their head bowed all the time.

* * *

Other great achievers have had the same struggle as Tyson Fury — people as different, on the surface, as Winston Churchill and Kurt Cobain. Churchill called his depression 'the Black Dog'.

John Connors is an Irish actor and traveller, best-known for his role in the Irish crime drama series *Love/Hate*. Connors is two years younger than Fury and has spoken about facing similar issues — hostility to his heritage, problems with depression and mental health, and the difficulty of reaching out.

> Being a traveller ain't helping me in the industry. It's also a class issue. I could count on one hand the working-class actors I know. You also have to kiss ass a lot and I don't do that, I just don't give a shit ... I try my best to advocate mental health for travellers, or anybody, I don't care who they are, and even I find it hard to talk about mental health, and I went through some really tough times, through depression. I still go through it, I still get it bad. It comes back to me. It's a

very Irish thing, but with travellers it's even more so because it's seen as a sign of weakness.

The suicide rate is over six times higher for traveller men compared to the general population of Ireland. Connors lost his own father to suicide when he was just eight-years-old. The actor believes the suicide rate among travellers won't change anytime soon because it's so deep-rooted.

> If you look at any people across the world who are suffering from racism, especially institutionalised racism, or any sort of oppression, there's a high suicide rate, because what happens from that is you internalise the hatred and you become ashamed. Travellers will tell you they're proud, and they are on the surface, but deep down a lot of them are ashamed. A stereotype gets created and then you become a self-fulfilling prophecy and that's what adds to the suicide rate.

* * *

When depression is really bad, it can feel like one of those dreams where you try to move, but every step and every motion feels like you're struggling to move through something heavy and viscous. Emotionally, it covers you completely, separating you from your motivation, your focus, and everything positive in life.

To keep itself strong and in charge, it tells you lies like, 'You are the worst at everything. Nobody really likes you. You don't deserve to be happy. This will never end.' ...And on, and on. You can't force it to go away. If you could just stop feeling unhappy, you would! But depression isn't just feeling unhappy. Really, it's a lot of things together that are most easily simplified into feeling unhappy.

Depression is a weight that holds you down in order to suck the life out of you — one which makes it a struggle to breathe in, without sucking back in the debris from your life. Then, once again, your worst enemy — your own thoughts — plant shadows through every part of your spirit. You want it to end.

The thought of not having to fight anymore brings you an unexpected amount of pleasure. Now you're almost anticipating the next attack because you want it to obliterate you into nothingness. Then you briefly see an opening to the other side, but something comes along and shuts the opening. It's not going to let you out. You're not done yet. You're thrown back on the battlefield. Another round will begin tomorrow...

* * *

Early in his career, Tyson Fury had been a strikingly handsome man, almost shy and diffident, with a soft, almost-lilting voice. His voice had now taken on the gravelly tone of his father's — and he had lost some of his hair — so that, at times, you could hardly tell the two apart. How had Tyson Fury suddenly become the battle-worn centurion, who looked so much older than the years that he now thought were done?

* * *

It's one of the clichés — or the eternal truths — of the martial artist's training that his greatest battle is always with himself. Tyson Fury, himself, said it: 'Who is the biggest opponent I've faced? ...Me.'

But gradually, there came the vaguest of hopeful signs that the emergency might now become an emergence. *'I'm going through a lot of personal demons, trying to shake them off,'* he said one Monday morning, adding that he'd been sober for three days — and that from the first of the month [two days before] he'd simply stopped taking all drugs and alcohol.

> *It does make me feel better. I've got to get me family back on track, get me wife back, you know. I've got to start doing things and manning up a bit, because there are a lot people out there, a lot worse off than*

> *me in life, and no matter how depressed I get, I've got three beautiful children here, and they've got a life and what would they do without a father? You gotta feel better 'cause you look at pure innocence and feel good. They don't know what's going on. It's not their fault. Listen if I never had kids, I wouldn't be alive today, that's the truth.*

But did he see any way for him fight back in terms of boxing? Coming from such a legendary fighting family, what had his victory meant to *them*?

> *Nothing can ever, ever mean more to my family, my history of people, than winning those titles. We are bare-knuckle champions, boxing champions — all that matters to us is fighting.*

The real fightback and his return from the brink of death began, ironically, symbolically, at a Halloween party, where he was dressed as a skeleton — which must have been some sight.

> *I was 29 — everyone else there was younger — and I thought, 'Is this what I want from my life?' No matter how many people had told me before that I needed to change my life, I'd never fully realized it. I left early and went home into a dark room, took the skeleton*

suit off and I prayed to God to help me. I'd never begged to God to help me. I could feel tears running down my face. I almost accepted that being an alcoholic was my fate but after praying for ten minutes, I got up I felt the weight was lifted off my shoulders. For the first time in my life I thought I was going to be OK. I just knew I couldn't do it on my own.

Later, Tyson Fury's brother, Shane, summed it all up:

> It's amazing that he came back from where he was. He wasn't just fat — and put a load of weight on — he was *down*. He was in a bad way — he was in a worse way than we thought because we didn't know what was going on. If you asked him, you never got anything from him. We'd say, 'You're a fool, you're seeking attention, you're a clown. Get your act together!' We'd just criticize him. But when he was going through what people [now] know, it was hard. A man needs goals. No matter what he's doing. Even if he doesn't need money — if he's helping someone else, whatever — you need a goal. And I think he knows now. That's what he's got to do.

Round 7

He's Back!

MERRY CHRISTMAS, GUYS. I'VE HAD A NIGHTMARE 2016, done a lot of stuff I'm not proud of, but my promise to you is I'll return in 2017,' tweeted Fury. He was back in training ahead of a ring return. Peter Fury announced that Tyson would be returning around springtime 2017, aiming for a fight against WBC champion Deontay Wilder, who would be making a voluntary defence.

Promoter Frank Warren spoke about possible opponents, adding that a court hearing was set for 8 May.

> I want to see him back in the ring as soon as possible, but before that happens he's got a couple of issues to sort out,' said Warren. 'I've got a lot of time for him ...I'd like to be involved in moving forward and getting

him back to where he should be, which is being the number one heavyweight.

But within hours of Fury announcing a comeback date, the British Boxing Board of Control's general secretary, Robert Smith, spoke out to say that Fury was still suspended and would most definitely not be fighting yet — adding that there'd been no contact from Fury nor his representatives since the ban had started. Fury said, in that case, he'd get a license through the Boxing Union of Ireland — although *they* claimed no application had been received.

On 25 April, Fury announced that he would make his ring return on the undercard of Billy Joe Saunders' world middleweight title defence on 8 July. Robert Smith again spoke up, saying that Fury's case had been adjourned, to be carried on later.

'It's still ongoing,' he said. 'This is one of those legal cases that go on a long time. I'm not surprised, it's not unusual — it's obviously a complex case. I'll expect a decision when I'm given it.'

After pulling himself round from a state of despair, Fury now found himself with neither an indefinite ban nor a date set to be able to return. In a state of limbo, with his licence still suspended, and no date set for the hearing, he begged for clarity on his situation. For the time being Tyson Fury could still only talk his talk rather than walk his walk.

> *To be honest I have to get some weight off, I've lost nearly two stone in two weeks so everything is going really well for me at the moment. I've really turned my life around and done a U-turn on everything and I'm feeling a lot better than I did before. I'm starting to get everything great again. I'm back enjoying the gym work and that's how it's supposed to be. I'm a long way from entering back in the ring but I'm on the right path. When I get my license back and I get fit again, and I get this five stone off.* [Although he probably needed to lose more like seven or eight stone] *...I think they are all bums. I reckon personally on my night in the heavyweight division I think I'm capable of beating anybody.*

Even at this earliest of stages, it was obvious that Fury now had his sights set on what would be the biggest heavyweight confrontation in British boxing history. When Tyson Fury said he feared nobody, everyone translated that into meaning Anthony Joshua. It was only going to be a matter of how quickly he could get his mojo back and how many warm-up fights he would need. While Fury was still waiting to face the charge for the alleged use of a prohibited substance, Joshua said he was expecting him to come back because he would find peace fighting again.

Tyson Fury claimed to be far from being impressed by Joshua's achievements, calling him 'a pumped-up weight-lifter'. And for all of Joshua's hand speed, precision, and impressive physique, you could see Fury's point. Joshua put many people in mind of another superbly-muscled British heavyweight, Frank Bruno — whose journey ended with his head bobbing around like a cork, and looking in danger of becoming completely detached, once Mike Tyson started giving it some serious attention.

Both Fury and Joshua were undefeated in their respective professional careers. As the saying has it: 'Someone's 'o', would have to go.' Joshua, too, appeared keen on the showdown, as he had called out Fury moments after Fury had secured his win against Klitschko. The one fight that everyone wanted to see was Fury v Joshua. Everything now hinged of the verdict of the UKAD. But there was further delay when the vital hearing was further postponed, following 'a conflict of interest' on its panel.

* * *

In the first week of December, 2017, Tyson Fury became a father-of-four. When Paris gave birth to a baby girl, the couple kept up the tradition of noteworthy names. Perhaps she got off lightly, compared to the three other children: Prince John James, Venezuela, and Prince Tyson Fury II. The arrival was announced on social media: *'My new angel Valencia Amber. The Lord has blessed me yet again'.*

It was only on 12 December 2017, that Tyson Fury finally became free to resume his boxing career. Just over two years since his victory against Klitschko, UKAD announced that Fury had been given a two-year ban. Crucially, the ban had been backdated to November 2015, which meant that Fury (and his cousin, Hughie) had already served the ban and were now free to fight again, subject to receiving a licence.

The two men once again claimed they'd never 'knowingly or deliberately committed any anti-doping rule violation' and accepted the backdated two-year ban. Both men blamed the result of the elevated drug levels on eating uncastrated wild boar. [It was a similar defence to the one used by Spanish cyclist and two-time Tour de France winner, Alberto Contador, who'd also tested positive for the banned steroid in 2010.]

> *I'm a fighting man through and through and I've never backed down from anyone in my life and I was certainly not going to back down from fighting this dispute. Hughie and I have maintained our innocence from day one and we're now happy that it has finally*

been settled with UKAD and that we can move forward knowing that we'll not be labelled drug cheats. I can now put the nightmare of the last two years behind me, which has been particularly hard on my family, but with their support and strength, we've fought through together and I can now enjoy Christmas with my family and new-born daughter. Next year I will be back doing what I do best, better than ever and ready to reclaim the world titles which are rightfully mine. It's time to get the party started.

The case had been complicated by the failure of the test for cocaine in September 2016. Fury admitted using the recreational drug to deal with depression related to injury and the UKAD problems. As part of the compromise deal, UKAD withdrew a charge against Fury of failure to provide a sample in September 2016. However, his February 2015 win over Christian Hammer was officially disqualified: 'All titles, prize money, and ranking points secured as a result of his victory in that fight are forfeited,' read the UKAD statement. The result of this fight would likely be changed officially to a 'no-contest'.

* * *

It's almost unbelievable now to think that during the first phase of his professional career, Team Fury was pretty much a family-run business. There were no sponsorship deals in place nor any merchandising. You couldn't buy a Tyson Fury T-shirt even if you wanted to. By November 2017, it was obvious that serious changes were happening behind the scenes. Word had it that Peter Fury would no longer be training Fury, nor Mick Hennessey acting as his promoter. Fury took a significant step toward making his ring return by signing with MTK Global, the fast-growing advisory and management company founded by Matthew Macklin (who himself made three thrilling middleweight world title shots in a brave career).

> *I couldn't be happier to sign with MTK Global. It is unbelievable how fast they have grown and what they have achieved in the past few years. I spoke to my friend Billy Joe Saunders and he only had good things to say about MTK, so it was an easy decision to go with them.*

'Fury is still the lineal heavyweight world champion because he never lost his belts in the ring,' said MTK director Paul Gibson. 'In many people's eyes Tyson is still the man in the heavyweight division. It is fantastic news for the sport that he is coming back to prove that fact in the ring.' Fury outlined plans for his comeback, saying he wanted to fight five opponents in 2018.

> *There is a lot of politics involved in boxing. It is not just two fighters getting in the ring and fighting.*

There is so much to do. That's all unimportant to me. Where it is, who it is, what date it is. As long as I get back out there in 2018, I'll be happy. I am itching to get back in there, and we are well in the planning stages. It's all starting to come together. I want to get four or five fights in next year. I'm ready for that amount.

* * *

As divisive a figure as he'd often been, only the most meanspirited of people would want to see a talent like Fury's wasted, or for him to throw his legacy away. With his licence suspended, Fury had ballooned to a massive twenty-seven stone, creating a significant chance that we might have seen the last of him. On more than one occasion, he'd announced his retirement. But something had persuaded him to fight it out. He got himself back in the gym and dedicated himself to a ketogenic diet. The excess weight started falling away till it was plain to see. One look at his face on his Instagram videos made it abundantly clear that Fury looked happier, healthier, and more focused.

He began teasing the announcement of his first fight since November 2015. In his two years away from the sport, he'd seen the likes of Anthony Joshua and Joseph Parker lift the belts that he'd never properly lost. While it might be several months before we saw Fury competing for titles again, he was coming back to reclaim them.

* * *

On the same day he was cleared by the British Boxing Board of Control to fight once again, Fury was appearing at an event — 'An Evening with Tyson Fury' — at the Marriott Hotel in Bristol. He appeared to be in good spirits during the event and even sang a Neil Diamond song on stage at the end of the evening.

After working on the event, a supplier, Daniel Fry, took his two children along to collect equipment when, much to the excitement of one of the boys, they spotted the heavyweight. Fry said his 7-year-old son Oliver, immediately ran up to him, very excited.

'I explained to Tyson he has autism, hence the bombardment of questions — which didn't faze Tyson at all — and he picked both my boys up and then started talking to them whilst I thought I'd capture the moment.'

A photo posted by Fry to Twitter showed Fury sitting with Oliver and his 3-year-old brother, Zachary, as they spoke about the fact they both have family in Manchester. Fry said his son was 'like a changed boy' after Fury sat and chatted with him for twenty minutes and described Fury as 'a complete gentleman'.

'All I can say is the moment they had was very special. It was a touching moment — Tyson didn't have to take the time with him that he did. He has definitely shown a different side to what's published in the media. He did a lot of autographs on the evening with photos for no fees at all. Everybody said how down to earth he was.'

* * *

HE'S BACK – THE REAL HEAVYWEIGHT CHAMPION OF THE WORLD.

...so read the banner behind Tyson Fury's press conference on 13 April 2018, to announce that he'd signed with the promoter Frank Warren, with the date of his first fight and the opponent yet to be announced.

Frank Warren:
> When he was having his problems, I texted him all the time. The world was watching. He was not living the life of a boxer — boozing and ballooning up. But I didn't realize it had got to the stage it he was at, *this* suicidal situation. I got in touch with him a few times and said, 'Listen, you need to come back. Try to do something with yourself. Come back in another capacity in boxing — train or manage a boxer.' To cut a long story short, we cut a deal and *his* fight became *my*

fight. I think he has to fight to keep himself there — and boxing has given him a direction and something to aim for. It's important to have self-esteem and feel good about yourself.

Frank Warren pointed out that Tyson Fury was still the lineal world champion and predicted he would return to prove himself the greatest heavyweight of his era. The first part of Warren's claim was valid — and there was more than a reasonable possibility that Fury could deliver on the second.

[A 'lineal champion' is traditionally regarded as 'the man who beat the man' in the heavyweight division that goes all the way back to 1885 and John L Sullivan. Whenever there's a break in the line (as there was when Lennox Lewis retired as the reigning champion), the two independent bodies who monitor the succession meet to confer the honour on the next man considered to be dominating the division. That was where Wladimir Klitscho came in, and stayed — until Fury upset the long-reigning Ukrainian.]

Fury's absence from the ring didn't negate his standing. Warren rightly argued that Fury still outranked Anthony Joshua, the holder of the WBA, IBF, WBO and IBO belts, and Deontay Wilder, the WBC champion

Frank Warren knew that proof wouldn't be established simply by Fury winning a fight against a relatively-safe handpicked opponent.

> AJ simply picked up the belts that Tyson left behind. He and Wilder are good heavyweights, but unless one of them beats Fury neither of them is the true world champion. Those fights have to happen.

> We're not stupid. All the great fighters who have been successful in comebacks have taken it step by step. It's a rebuilding process. It takes time to get the timing back in the ring and to prove yourself, not only physically but mentally. When you hit rock bottom like that, you have to climb back by baring your soul. That

takes courage and Tyson has done it. Now he will be the greatest heavyweight of his generation.

I was a doubter once and I made that clear when I said I expected Dereck Chisora to beat him. But Tyson played with Dereck, who didn't win one second of any round. Tyson's exceptional boxing brain is still there. He is sharp and he still has his hand speed. The only thing that could let him down is his legs but I see no sign that his legs are gone. I no longer doubt that he will beat every other top heavyweight in the world as soon as he's ready.'

I've just set myself a goal of beating the great Joe Louis' record of 25 title defences. Wladimir Klitschko almost beat Joe Louis' record [which included 66 victories in 69 professional bouts, as he reigned supreme in the heavyweight division from 1937 to 1949.] *If I have three fights a year, I've beaten him. It's a hard challenge but I've never set a challenge I didn't make. If anyone is capable of doing it, I'm capable.*

But the media weren't that easily persuaded and still had tabloid sensation on their mind. The *ITV News* reporter, Nick Wallis, caught up with Fury after the press conference...

You've said things in the past that people have found abhorrent —

Fury cut him off before the question could be completed showing how he was now going to handle things.

Don't even go there.

Wallis persisted.

...Boxing, please. I'm a boxer. I'm not interested in politics or anything else.

Wallis then tried to question Fury on his ban from the sport.

...Terminated.

Fury turned and walked away.

* * *

At the beginning of May, Fury appeared on *Good Morning TV* to be interviewed by a slightly more deferential Piers Morgan.

To what do you attribute your ability to lose weight so fast, and get back into game mode?

> *Basically I just have a low-carb diet and train really hard. I do get hungry but I think to myself, 'Do I want to look really fat in the morning?' I'm feeling good,*

> *I'm just happy to be back involved in the sport. It's almost like I've got a second career.*

There's one fight that everyone wants to see — Anthony Joshua against Tyson Fury. Now, you've seen Joshua — he's a magnificent athlete, he's a great boxer, he's got heart. Do you think you have the tools to beat him? You've got the heart, the guts, but do you think you have the tools to beat Joshua?

> *Of course, I do. I wouldn't be sitting here today – I'd be out in Spain drinking sangrias. Of course I have the ability. I just have too much movement and natural boxing skill to lose to somebody like that. He's tough and strong and has a lot of 'learned' ability, but he doesn't have the natural gift ...the sweet science ...He knows and everyone in boxing knows who the real champion is. I'm not here to discredit anyone – I will prove it.*

Was there 'a light bulb' moment in whatever it was you went through?

> *I always felt that the light switch was there. I thought, 'It's two and half years, I'd better flip this switch now, because it's been kind of a long time and I'd better do it soon.' I thought when I'm ready I'll know it deep inside. And that day came...*

* * *

On 20 May it was confirmed that Tyson Fury would launch his return to the ring on 9 June against the Albanian, Sefer Seferi. . It was clear that no risks were being taken. Although Seferi, 39, had been significantly more active than Fury, and had lost only once at heavyweight (against Manuel Charr in September 2016), he was essentially a career cruiserweight. But he was exactly the type of opponent Fury and his new promoter, Frank Warren, were targeting.

Fury went into the fight at odds of anything between 1/40 and 1/1000 favourite [meaning, you would need to stake £1000 to win £1]. Fury and Warren were planning for at least two more fights before the end of 2018. It would be in 2019 that they would target higher-profile and more-dangerous fights, once Seferi and other 'keep-busy' opponents had been overcome.

As he did for his fight against Klitschko, Fury once again trained with kickboxer Rico Verhoeven, who (probably with a little prompting from Frank Warren) believed the Gyspy King had everything it took to get back to the top, and be the best in the heavyweight division.

> He can be the very best, in my opinion. I've been training with the guy for years and years, I've seen him

grow. I've seen him go through ups and downs and he just has something special. He can fight orthodox or southpaw. He's so big, but he moves so easy. All the other contenders see that. He's got quick hands, he can take a punch but he can give a punch too. Look how he played with Vladimir Klitschko — Klitschko couldn't land a punch. That's what I do in my sport – I fight my opponent but I also make them fight themselves. Scramble their minds. Make them think all the time 'What the hell do I do here? I just can't touch this guy so I just go in.' And that's when they get hit. That's what Fury does too.

Seferi was expected to be durable without posing a significant threat, giving Fury a good workout over the course of their scheduled ten rounds — and a chance to shed some of the ring-rust that had accumulated. He would also be the first opponent since Fury had begun working with new trainer Ben Davison, following a split from his uncle, Peter Fury.

Round 8

Fighting Weight

TYSON FURY ONCE SAID THAT HE WOULD GIVE UP IF HIS uncle ever abandoned his corner: *'If I wasn't with Peter, I wouldn't be in boxing. I wouldn't train with anyone else.'* He hailed his uncle as his guardian angel.

Yet Tyson Fury's 'guardian angel' was once one of Britain's most-feared crime lords. An investigation by the *Sunday People* revealed how the 47-year-old trainer was a convicted kingpin at the heart of the gangland drugs scene who'd set up a business in an industrial unit, imported pure amphetamine from Belgium, 'cut' it, and distributed it around the North West. In 1995, he was jailed for ten years for possession and intent to supply, but continued to orchestrate his business from behind bars. In 2008, he got another two years for drug-related money laundering. In 2012, a court ordered Peter Fury to pay back the assets and funds he had hidden from the court.

The permatanned trainer was known for his love of Ferraris and Porsches and had the personalised plate PPF1. He'd bought a Porsche 911 for £63,000 cash while still living in a caravan. He posted a Twitter picture of himself outside his Cannes villa, standing with a black McLaren 570S Coupe sports car that cost £144,000, giving a thumbs-up, with the coy caption: 'Wonder who's just bought this super machine?' A better caption might have been: 'Selling speed to buy speed.'

A court once described Peter Fury as 'a man of considerable intelligence' who'd set up a complex business network using twelve different names and accounts in America, Jersey, the Isle of Man, Spain, Belgium, and Ireland. Throughout, he'd continued to insist that he made his money by car dealing, boxing, and bare-knuckle fighting. Following his convictions, he was ordered to pay back the best part of £1m to UK authorities, or face another four years behind bars – and then still repay the full amount on his release. A spokesman for the National Crime Agency said: 'Peter Fury paid the full amount back to the court and complied with an order requiring him to submit all his financial details for nine years.'

Peter Fury told *Boxing Monthly*, 'I've just finished paying nearly a million quid to the Government, insisting that he'd gone straight, and that his current wealth was from legitimate business. 'Now I have to *show* people that I don't get into anything. I'm a recluse, really. The police have a lot of informants and intelligence, so they know I'm not active in anything. I'm happy with that.' He claimed training Tyson and his son Hughie (who later became English heavyweight champion) had helped him sort out his life and given him fresh focus.

Peter Fury claimed he'd been was sucked into criminality. He told the Internet blog *Boxing Scene.com*: 'I was wild when I was younger. I'd see someone with a nice pair of trainers on and want to have a fight with them. Then, anyone who wanted protection would come to me because I was seen as a tough young fella. One thing led to another. I went from looking after people, to looking after areas, to looking after cities.'

Tyson said he and his uncle were a great team...

We have been big influences in each other's lives. Without Peter, I wouldn't be in this position today and without me, he wouldn't be either. We have been like guardian angels for each other. It works and we are a close unit.

So what prompted Tyson Fury to switch trainers to Ben Davison?

At the time that Fury relinquished his world titles, lost his boxing licences, and announced his retirement, he blasted Peter Fury for 'jumping in bed with the enemy' — and uploaded a photo to Instagram showing Peter and promoter Mick Hennessy in David Haye's gym, with Haye's manager Adam Morallee in the middle. Peter Fury was seen shaking Morallee's hand, while Hennessy had his arm around his shoulder. It's believed he was there to negotiate a potential fight between Hughie Fury and Haye — provided Hughie defeated Joseph Parker to win the WBO world title. Peter Fury posted on Twitter saying a deal had been agreed — while Haye posted saying he was well on his way to a ring return after the shoulder surgery that forced him to pull out of the February 2014 fight with Tyson.

Tyson captioned his own photo: *'Can't believe you're both in that prick's gym and even considering doing business with that piece of shit. I'm totally disappointed in you both.*

Despite all of that, John Fury was always grateful to Peter for looking after Tyson at the time that John still had some months left to serve in prison.

* * *

The youthful Ben Davison may not have looked as battle-hardened as some of boxing's old-school trainers, but he watched every punch of the eleven workouts a week he oversaw that succeeded in cutting seven stones off the former world champion. As he recalls...

> I'd met Tyson once or twice and I knew what sort of character he was and what he was going through at the time. When he came over I thought, 'He's not interested in boxing.' But I thought it would be a bit of company for Billy Joe [Saunders] through the two

week training camp we were doing. I remember roughing him up — we got gloved up and we got in the ring, and I remember he just stood there, looked at me, and laughed. He was so happy to start doing a bit of training. That's when I thought, 'Maybe he does want to come back. Maybe he still has a love for the sport.

But, at first, when he came into the gym, he would blow hot and cold. So I thought, 'My main goal at the minute, before getting him back into condition, is getting his love back for the sport — enjoying it and *wanting* to train. Because we knew how long it would take — it was a mammoth task — it was 'mission impossible'. To be honest, I would sit on the sidelines thinking, 'I don't know if this job can be done.'

But we both took a risk with each other. I had a gym back home — I had family back home — I had things going well back home. I had to take a risk on whether he was going to commit to it and go through the mammoth task and the hard, hard work it would be. I had to trust he was going to do that. And he had to trust me to give him the level that we needed.

I've spent time around a lot of top, top trainers — and invaluable time of experience — I knew when to push him and when not. I knew the signs when he was starting to fatigue. I knew when he was going to be sore, and when not. I knew when to take my foot off the pedal and when to put my foot on the pedal. That was my job — to make sure it was a good balance — that he enjoyed it and that the work was getting done.

We got on and gelled straight away — outside of the gym, in the gym, my coaching style, his fighting style. At the beginning it really *was* mission impossible. No-one believed we could do it — or that anyone could do it. That shows how much dedication he put in.

When I took the job on, I knew we needed to get him to Marbella and get away from all the distractions so he could focus on what we were doing. It was a must. I knew the good weather would help him and that was the first stage of getting him back into his routine. My goal at that stage was to get him back in love with boxing.

He decided to drive over there at the last minute, as opposed to flying, for some strange reason, but that's how Tyson is. The drive was about thirty hours and there were a few points where he wanted to turn back, but we got him there in the end and he's been in good spirits ever since. Paris and the kids were with us, and Hughie came out to join us. It was important to have them there because if we were just constantly working, I believe it wouldn't have worked. It was good to have that support from his family at the start because they drive him on — and it worked perfectly.

* * *

Beyond Fury needing to drop weight dramatically, a vital part of this training camp was keeping his mind on an even keel. To that end, Fury briefly enlisted the support of snooker star, Ronnie O'Sullivan — someone who's had his own fight with depression and lack of motivation. Maybe O'Sullivan introduced Fury to his own mentor, the celebrity sports psychologist, Dr Steve Peters — the man famous for getting athletes and sportsmen to overcome what he calls their 'inner chimp', and focus their energies.

Ben Davison also took over monitoring Fury's social media accounts to prevent things going astray — lest Tyson embark on one of his stream-of-consciousness accusations or confessionals. Fury was beginning to look a lot further on from the man in the *Rolling Stone* interview of two years earlier. Ben Davison believed that they had somehow found the key to unlocking his potential.

> Everybody needs routine and structure and that was a big part of Tyson's life until he stopped fighting and lost those elements. The key is to keep him mentally stimulated. If you allow him to get bored or switch off, he can do that very easily. I've not allowed him to do that in this camp and I worked it out pretty quickly. I gave him set training times, set meal times, and the more he got into that routine, I found him getting

better each day. The weight was coming off and he was looking better in the gym.

To help Fury shed seven stone, nutritionist Greg Marriott was responsible for designing a diet, consisting of high amounts of fat, moderate protein, and low carbohydrate. A ketogenic diet is a low-carb diet that produces ketones in the liver which are used as energy. By lowering the intake of carbs, the body is induced into a state called ketosis which helps it survive when food intake is low. Burning ketones as the primary energy source helps you lose weight, while there are also other physical and mental benefits. A typical breakfast would be rye bread, avocado, eggs, and lean bacon. He would avoid all foods containing sugars.

'We give him high-glycaemic gel, like cyclists use,' said Marriott, 'which powers him through an hour training session. When he's done an hour's session, the carbohydrate is out of his body, he utilises a different fuel source which burns fat.'

Ben Davison held two training sessions a day between Monday and Friday, with one on a Saturday. Crucially, work was not only about making the big man sweat but on nourishing his active mind.

I broke it into two camps. The first one was getting the majority of the weight off, but then he needed to recover. The first phase was making sure his body was ready to go through what was needed to get where he is now. There was a lot of cardio but he also needed to prepare the tendons, the ligaments, almost like injury-prevention training. That's high repetition stuff, low weights, long duration, with light intensity, and as the body adapts to the intensity we increase, increase, increase.

In sparring, I might say to him, 'You're only allowed to counter-punch with two shots', or 'You're only allowed to use your left hand'. It keeps him switched on with a target in mind and that's how you get the best out of Tyson. You have to alleviate boredom. Fury is a happy man, now. I'm not really proud of myself, I'm proud of him. He has put the work in and done everything he has had to do. To lose that amount of weight alone shows how dedicated he has been.

The question now was, 'Would this meticulous planning help Fury regain the form that saw him outbox Klitschko in his Dusseldorf coronation?'

It definitely will. He's very heavy-handed, but at this same time his movement and footwork is very slick.

> He's got two V12 engines in him to go the distance and when all those skills are firing and working together, it's going to take a very good man to beat him.

It was still too early to suggest what might happen in a fight between Fury and Joshua, but Ben Davison thought 2019 might be an appropriate time to hold that conversation.

> That would be the right time for Tyson to be looking at a heavyweight world title unification clash. We have a set plan to get to that fight. But that is ideally when we'll be looking at a summer showdown and filling out a stadium.

But that was for the future. For now Ben Davison could only reflect on how far they'd just come...

> It makes the hair on the back of my neck stand up talking about it, because nobody could ever know the deepness and the truth of the journey. I just wanted to see the man back happy and enjoying life again. And from the position he was in, to where he is now, is unexplainable. There's no way I could ever come out with it ... He's probably saved thousands of people that he doesn't even know about. The fact that he's open and talks about it, and gives people inspiration — that's bigger than anything.

Fury shed excess weight equivalent to the *entire* weight of the man behind him... Ricky Hatton.

* * *

It's not unusual for a boxer or an entertainer's career to suddenly collapse, like Fury's did. What *is* rare is for someone to regain their former status. Ali was denied the opportunity to fight, but he never stopped training for three years. Fury came back from an altogether deeper place, but he showed that he'd now 'got it'.

> *When the boxing's done, I'll continue to train — and that will keep me well, mentally and physically. I thought it was the boxing, but I've realized it's the training. It took me a long time to figure that out. Twenty years.*

Long-term goals and talk of potential super-fights could begin to make headlines and fuel gossip. But for now, Fury could simply return to the ring a relatively fit and happy man. That itself had to be a something of a victory.

Round 9

The First Step

THE 39-YEAR-OLD SEFER SEFERI WAS A HUGE UNDERDOG but Tyson Fury insisted he wouldn't be underestimating him.

I'm taking him deadly serious. This is a world-title fight for me. Every one of these people who come to fight me is challenging me for my lineal heavyweight status. I think he's good ... Any man who's had 24 fights and only lost one on points, and never been knocked out, can't be a pushover. Try punching someone and knocking them out — it's quite hard. He'll be able to punch no doubt. A chin is a chin, and if he hits me on mine, I'll go over. But if I'm as good as I think I am, I should beat him comfortably. If I'm useless, I'll lose and you can't say fairer than that.

Fury said that Seferi was selected as his opponent because of his durability, adding that he needed to be tested after a lengthy period of inactivity, to shake off the ring rust.

> *These Albanian fellas are very, very tough. That's why I picked someone who is very tough. I need the rounds because I've been out for a long time. I don't need a knockout after ten seconds. I need someone who can take the punches and can keep coming forward and put me under pressure.*

One of Fury's sparring partners, Tom Little, said he had never worked with anyone as unpredictable as Fury in the ring.

> I'm good at making people miss, but I make him miss and then he hits me where I have moved to. He has the best timing I have ever seen. When you stand in front of him you soon find out how good he is. He's the real deal. Tyson understands big punchers get knocked out all the time. They get vulnerable as they are putting so much into that shot. Tyson doesn't load up until he knows he has someone. He's a safety-first fighter. Boxing is about winning and that's what he is good at doing. I hope we see a massive showdown and he can burst the Joshua hype-train.

*   *   *

On the Tuesday night, four days before the fight, Tyson Fury had just finished an open workout at the National Football Museum, in Manchester, when he headed to a Nando's chicken restaurant. After enjoying a meal with his team, Fury settled the tab for all those in the restaurant — paying around £700 for all the other fifty-two. They followed him — eventually in their hundreds, with Shane on his right shoulder and John on his left — all the way back to his hotel, singing choruses of *Walking in a Fury Wonderland*.

On the day of the fight, Fury posted a training video made at Ricky Hatton's gym in Hyde. He looked sharp, focussed, and accurate while sparring, occasionally breaking away to talk to camera.

> *If I can't annihilate this division — this weak, poor division — with no boxers in it at all, then I must be useless myself. They're a pack of bums. AJ can't box — he couldn't even do nothing with Joseph Parker, and he's just a poor man's Tyson Fury ...no disrespect Joseph. Deontay Wilder... what's he gonna do, follow me around the ring all day, looking to land a punch? And if he can't land it, he's totally fucked, isn't he. If I'm any good at all I'll come back and I'll wipe 'em all out. An' if I'm completely rubbish useless, I'll lose*

won't I? I'll never be able to show my face in public ever again. I'll never be able to call myself the Gypsy King anymore through losing to a weightlifter and a football player. It's not happening is it?

Pacing the ring and sweating, he looked in to the mood to fight...

There's never been anyone like me before... six foot nine — shit-kicking, cow-punching banger. I can't be stopped. Watch this round.

He was moving like a super-middleweight, and he knew it...

...'Ever seen that before from a heavyweight? I've been born and bred to fight. These guys have come to box one night. Wilder started boxing at 20-odd-year-old — Joshua's the same. I've been doing it from a little child. So, if I can't give them a boxing lesson, show them how sweet science works, and strip all the titles off them.

...Because if I can't beat them, I don't ever want to class myself as a world champion. If I can't beat these men very easily, and make it look easy, then I must've never been any good anyway. I must've have fluked

it. How are you gonna let a fat man beat you? No pressure boys.

I'm like a chameleon...
I can adapt to any situation...
Any colour, any environment...
I'd come out a legend and a king.
Put me in the jungle, I'll be a ruler.
Put me in space, I'll own the place.
Put me anywhere in the world...
I am the Gypsy King.
Remember the name.

* * *

After a break of 925 days, Tyson Fury was back in the boxing ring. 'It is a Night of Sound and Fury' boomed out as he was announced. A roar went up from the crowd, many of who believed that he was still the rightful heavyweight champion of the world. During the ring walk, the Monkees' song *Daydream Believer* thundered out of the PA system. Though most of the crowd ignored the original *Cheer Up Sleepy Jean* chorus and went with the Manchester United football chant about Liverpool: 'Cheer up Kevin Keegan, Oh what can it mean? To a sad Geordie bastard. And a shite football team.'

Seferi's kit had 'Easy Motion Skin' logos emblazoned all over it. [You don't always associate heavyweights with moisturiser endorsements.] Fury looked like he could still drop a couple more stone. As the referee Phil Edwards gave them both their instructions, Fury leant forward and kissed Seferi on the head.

The fight itself was what we all knew it would be — a one-sided return to action against an opponent who was five stones lighter than him. All Fury wanted was rounds under his belt ...and maybe a knockout finish.

It began predictably, with Seferi circling on the outside. Fury landed a pair of fast jabs and a body shot, but spent more time showboating, laughing, and lifting his arms in the air in the 'come on then' gesture familiar to any self-respecting football hooligan — and which you have the liberty to do with a height advantage of nearly a foot. He did an Ali shuffle. Seferi did the same. Neither fighter could help laughing. There was more clowning until a second jab rocked the Albanian's head back. Whenever Fury landed, Seferi hung on to buy time. At the end of the round a short flurry of fast hands gave us a glimpse of the old Fury.

In the second round Fury was again playing to the crowd. It felt a little odd — as if he felt he had to live up to the entertaining joker version of himself. He was warned by the referee for looking to friends ringside: 'People have come to see a fight!' For the first time, Fury switched to southpaw. But the two men in the ring became distracted by a fight that had broken out in the crowd not far from one of the neutral corners. A few people tweeted that the better fight was going on outside the ring.

In the third, Fury rocked Seferi with a long straight right then, later in the round, landed a right uppercut and cuffing right hook. For the first time it looked like he was throwing off the ring rust.

By the fourth, Fury was unleashing heavy shots. For the first time in the fight Seferi was wobbling, as Fury looked as if he was now waiting to land that one killer punch. If he let his hands go and stopped playing the clown this would be all over.

It became apparent that Fury could've ended the fight whenever he wanted — but the decision was taken out of his hands by Seferi's corner as they pulled their man out. As there wasn't any serious injury, it was a bit of a let-down for all involved — not least the paying spectators. But had the fight continued there might well have been serious injury. With a few 'boos' ringing down from the upper tiers, it was hardly the victorious homecoming Fury had in mind — but much more relevant contests were sure to follow.

It was like I was having my debut again. It has been a long time out of the ring. There's still work to do. Frank Warren will keep me busy and the calibre of the opponents will keep on rising. I'm aiming to have a title shot by the end of the year.

The fight proved very little. Would it have helped if Seferi had been five inches taller and three stone heavier? Of course. But he wasn't there other than to throw a few punches and end up on the canvas. This was simply fight number one — not a competitive fight, simply the business of reintroducing Tyson Fury to an audience, and to his trade.

In the scheme of things, it was only the first step on Fury's road to redemption. All eyes would be on Frank Warren to come up with a sterner test next time up. The promoter confirmed that Fury would next box on the undercard of Carl Frampton's contest at Windsor Park, Belfast, on 18 August. There was talk of going for Tony Bellew before the end of the year.

* * *

If Fury were a Formula 1 car, the mechanic's assessment might go like this: 'Well boss, we've just rebuilt the engine, but without tuning it up. It's still covered in grease, but we did a test lap anyway. We didn't break the lap record, but we're not recommending scrapping it.'

We wouldn't really be able to assess Fury until after at least a couple more fights, when the muscle snap had returned and the remnants of fat had burned off. There were those that would've preferred to see Fury take on a top fighter and lose, simply to justify their vitriol and remove the embarrassment they still carried from their posts, comments, and articles pre-Klitschko.

Considering that many doubted that Fury would ever make it back to the ring at all, given a little time, he might yet provide more big fight nights. It might well be that Fury had really needed his 925-day break, both mentally and physically to let himself go. As he has said, he'd been boxing from the age of ten. And it was immediately after he'd won the ABA final in 2008, that father John appeared on his son's shoulder and told everybody that this young man would be heavyweight champion of the world. Many scoffed, but it underlined the kind of pressure that was being put on him even then.

Fury's performance against Klitschko (which he said was him boxing at only fifty percent of his potential) would give any heavyweight in the world a problem. But Wilder and Joshua were younger than Klitschko. It was the intriguing uncertainty around what might happen next that was drawing us back in.

Could Joshua keep chasing Fury, hitting him with jabs or right hands? Could he ever get near him? With Wilder, would Tyson get clipped by one good right hand? Of course, the Fury who beat Klitschko should be able to beat Joshua or Wilder. The question was: 'Were we going to see *him* again?'

Round 10

Future Prospect

TYSON FURY'S 'OLD-TESTAMENT' VIEWS AND COMMENTS made him the BBC's 'Public Enemy Number One' for a while. But many appreciated Fury's honesty. When so many people in the public eye are manufactured and scripted, Fury was anything but. What you saw was what you got — though he did tend to say whatever came into his head — and he *did* like talking. If you were a politically-correct liberal, he was a nightmare. But he was also authentic, funny, and strangely likeable, and people responded to that. Some of his problems he'd brought on himself — but he'd held his hands up to that. And when all was said and done, most people could see that he only wanted a fair crack at the whip. He was a talented fighter, and a decent fella, and was to be welcomed back into the heavyweight mix.

* * *

Speaking before the Seferi fight, Matthew Macklin said that, on his comeback trail toward the biggest fight in history, Tyson Fury should battle Tony Bellew — adding that the clash would tee up the Anthony Joshua fight perfectly.

> Anthony Joshua's stardom is sky high, selling out Wembley and Cardiff twice. I think the heavyweight division has caught fire since then. Tyson has been unfortunate in not being a part of the scene; he must have been on the side lines in absolute frustration.

Earlier in the year, Anthony Joshua told *Sky Sports*:

> Tyson Fury believes he is the best. And, in beating Wladimir Klitschko, he is the man who beat the man, when he was the man — and you cannot really argue about that. Joshua versus Fury — if it can happen down the line — will probably be the biggest fight of all time. But Tyson cannot walk back into a world title fight. Someone like Tony Bellew would not be a bad fight. Bellew has been very active and in big fights. If he comes through against David Haye again [which he later did], then maybe that fight makes sense for Tony Bellew, and it

certainly makes sense for Fury. The Bellew fight would sell.

* * *

So things were OK in the Joshua camp, for now, but the perception for many was already that Joshua's promoter Eddie Hearn would dodge Fury for as long as they could. And before Fury v Joshua could happen, Anthony Joshua would face other opponents. And Joshua beating *them* was not a given.

The perception was also that Joshua had been nursed through his early career by various means — including being very selective with opponents and having the help of some sympathetic refereeing. His one real test, when he beat Klitscho, was an odd affair. Klitschko had Joshua on the canvas, yet appeared to take it easy with him so that Joshua was able to recover to win the fight.

The hard-hitting American, Deontay Wilder, 32, had been locked in ongoing talks with Joshua's team for several weeks, with Eddie Hearn holding the stubborn view that the event should happen in the UK. Initially, Wilder said he would only put pen to paper if the fight was in the US, but now it appeared he was ready to take the challenge anywhere.

Taking on Instagram, he said:

> 'You don't see no fear in my eyes. I ain't scared of no man, I wasn't raised like that. This is what I do. No man can ever say he looked into my eyes and saw fear ... Dear Anthony Joshua fans, since you're acting dumb, delusional, or just plain stupid here you go ... Breaking News! ... The $50m offer for Joshua to fight me next in the US is still available to him if he wants it. In addition to that, today I agreed to their offer to fight Joshua next in the UK. If Joshua prefers the fight in the UK, the ball is in their court. It's up to them to choose, US or UK, I'm in.

Should the bout have happened, it would've seen all four of the major heavyweight titles on the line. But it seemed that Joshua's management were suddenly keen on exploring other avenues, as it was revealed he would most likely look to fight the Russian, Alexander Povetkin.

* * *

As for Fury's next immediate opponent — after another preparatory fight was scheduled for 18 August — one name that kept coming up was David Price, who seemed a viable candidate, if Fury was to step up the calibre of his opponents. Fury said that Price (who beat him as an amateur) was still possibly the biggest puncher among the British heavyweights.

'I'd throw my name into the hat,' said Price, the 34-year-old former British champion who stands six-foot-eight.

Price said he believed Fury needed to lose a further fifteen to twenty pounds, and looked really slow on his feet.

'Fury has a lot of work to do ... I can never remember people being blown away by Tyson Fury but he always finds a way to win. I think whoever you put in front of him ... it's tough to bet against him.'

In 2006, when Price was a highly-regarded Olympic bronze medallist with a pro record of 7–0, he'd outpointed Fury in the amateur ranks. Many thought Price would repeat that outcome as pros, if they met. And now there was talk of exactly that.

Tony Bellew — a career cruiserweight who'd only fought twice at heavyweight — would arguably pose too great a threat at this stage, given his two recent wins over David Haye, and might be deemed too much of a risk if Fury wanted to position himself for a world-title shot. [Later that year, on 11 November, Bellew suffered a devastating knockout defeat against Oleksandr Usyk, and announced his immediate retirement from boxing.]

The quickness of Fury's win over Seferi made it harder to discern what he'd retained or lost since 2015. As one ringside pundit said:

> Tyson Fury has a lot to address when he gets back in to the gym. I don't think he was concentrating when the fight began. He's tough to judge on that performance. It was a show rather than a fight. There's lots of work to do, and I think it will be four or five fights until we see the Tyson of old. I think Tyson Fury would be better, more switched-on, if he was up against someone he respected more. Someone he knew could hurt him. He'll be pleased to get this one out of the way though.

* * *

Fury's showing against Klitschko was used by many as a reference point in predicting the outcome of a clash with Joshua. The theory was that Fury's footwork and his ability to read opponents' intentions would leave Joshua connecting with shadows. But how much of that natural instinct remained? And would Joshua be a more accomplished operator now? They were only fourteen months apart in age, but they were separated by a gulf in personality, and in fighting styles.

And there was the connection forged at Finchley ABC — one that only they could truly evaluate. At the time, in September 2010, Fury spoke to boxing pundit Steve Bunce'

> *I tell you what; he's very, very good. Watch out for that name, Anthony Joshua, he's a prospect for the future.*

Now, as he mapped out his comeback, recalling those comments in more detail added to an already-compelling narrative for any showdown between the one-time sparring partners. It also reminded us how, on the trail to glory, fighters' journeys become so interwoven. Their exchanges, long ago, at Finchley Amateur Boxing Club in north London, were destined to be revived and scrutinised in much greater detail.

Back then, Joshua had just won the first of his two ABA national titles, and was in contention to represent England at the Commonwealth Games in India. Fury, was unbeaten in eleven professional fights and in need of quality sparring. He left his home in Lancaster and ventured to London where he met Joshua....

> *I thought to myself, 'I'm gonna take it easy cos he's only an amateur and he probably won't spar with me again if I go mad' ... He rushed*

> *at me, threw a one-two and a left hook and I tried to slip and slide and I thought, 'Ah, he's not so good, I'm gonna take my time'. And then 'Bash!' He hit me with a big uppercut on the point of the chin. If I'd have had a bit of a weak chin like David Price, I'd have been knocked out for a month.*

The uppercut Fury referred to became one of Joshua's calling cards and what brought about the end of Dillian Whyte, in 2015, to set up Joshua's own clash with Klitschko. But being mindful of the fact that they might bump into each other in the future, Fury went on to add that he then slowed Joshua down with a few body shots.

> *He had a good couple of rounds then I started hitting him round the body. He was like this, lifting his legs up in the corner, there were ten people in the gym who saw it ... Sparring ain't fighting. And sparring with a head guard on is not professional boxing, is it?* [Fury himself never wears a head guard when sparring.]

In only his third amateur contest, Joshua was floored and outpointed by the more-experienced Dillian Whyte, who gleefully reminded everyone of the fact in the build-up to their subsequent meeting in the pro ring. But at the O2 Arena in

London, it was Joshua who prevailed with a wicked uppercut finish in the 7th round. Coming just two weeks after Fury's masterful world-title-winning performance against Klitschko, that night marked the start of the increasing clamour of calls for a Fury-Joshua shootout.

One day soon?

* * *

On 12 July, it was announced that Tyson Fury's second comeback fight would be against the two-time world heavyweight title challenger, the Italian, Francesco Pianeta, at Belfast's Windsor Park, on 18 August.

It would be a step up in class from Sefer Seferi. At 6-foot-5, at least Pianeta was only four inches shorter than Fury. Ranked at 138th in the world, the German-based southpaw had twenty-one knockout wins on his record of 35-4-1, but had fallen short in his own challenges against Wladimir Klitschko. The Seferi fight was already history and Pianeta was a far better operator — his level of opposition told you that. But, for Fury, it was nothing more than a further move to get 'rounds under his belt' before moving on to the next level. Pianeta didn't seem to show much ambition of creating an upset on his own behalf.

The first section of Fury's ring-walk was accompanied by Rihanna's *'Live Your Life'*. But as he neared the ring, this changed to Lynyrd Skynyrd's *'Sweet Home Alabama'*. Deontay Wilder, who hailed from that part of the US, was present at ringside and recording this on his phone.

The Seferi fight had descended into a bit of a farce, with the Albanian retiring injured and Fury playing up to the crowd for laughs. This time Fury maintained an eagle-eyed focus for the entire contest. It was a night on which he ticked all the essential boxes and moved himself a little closer to fulfilling his ambition of reclaiming his world title belts after the best part of three years out.

With Ricky Hatton, Billy Joe Saunders, and Ben Davison in his corner, Fury moved through the gears, looking agile, flashing out his jab, and showing the footwork which he possessed in spite of his height and weight.

Round 1: As the bell sounded, Fury almost broke into a jog to get at Pianeta. He was up on his toes, and put his hands on the ropes to tempt Pianeta into throwing a few shots. The Italian didn't quite land, as Fury moved comfortably behind his jab. Fury was taking stock and didn't look interested in an early KO.

Round 2: There'd been no fooling around from Fury so far, no playing up to the cameras. He looked better on his feet — the benefit of shedding a further 18lbs since June. His reflexes looked sharp and he was seeing Pianeta's punches from a mile away.

Round 3: Fury started to combine punches, but took a right hand from Pianeta against the ropes at the close of the round. But there was still no doubt that Fury had won the first three rounds.

Round 4: Fury started to move through the gears and landed a good left hook. He was agile and accurate, moving well, and staying calm in another strong three minutes of boxing.

Round 5: Suddenly, rain was lashing down on the sections of the crowd who must surely have paid enough to be under cover. Waterproof ponchos were thrown down to them. This time, ignoring what was going on outside the ring, Fury maintained his focus. Wilder said he was impressed.

Round 6: Fury now started throwing his considerable weight around, leaning in on Pianeta and boring into him with his shaved head, wearing him down. Fury was still dropping his hands but his opponent couldn't capitalize. Ben Davison told Fury to stay patient and not walk onto anything silly.

Round 7: Fury caught Pianeta with a borderline punch. The Italian was given time out to recover. There was a lovely right hand from Fury and Pianeta looked like he was starting to tire and unravel as he gulped down air in the clinches.

Round 8: Fury landed a solid left hand to the head, and could have pushed for a stoppage. The rain was biblical now, lashing down in sheets.

Round 9: It hadn't been exhilarating, but Fury looked to be heading to a Las Vegas date with WBC champion Deontay Wilder. In the dying seconds, Fury caught Pianeta with a left hand.

Round 10: Fury had switched to southpaw in the final two rounds, and was cruising through the last three minutes at arm's length. He had thoroughly out-boxed his man tonight. David Haye said that Fury had been holding back because Wilder was ringside and he didn't want to reveal his full bag of tricks.

We awaited the formality of the points' decision. There were some half-hearted 'boos' from the Belfast crowd who'd been hoping for a KO. Apart from being backed up in the corner once, Fury looked comfortable as he was taken the distance. It even looked as if his opponent may have been asked to try and take Fury the distance. Pianeta never really fought in earnest, but did enough to survive. He was simply there to provide the right test at the right time. Fury's performance had few frills, yet few mistakes. Referee Steve Gray scored every round in favour of Fury, raising his record to twenty-seven victories without defeat.

* * *

Following the win, Deontay Wilder, working ringside with US broadcasters *Showtime*, climbed through the ropes and stepped into the ring for the customary confrontation. The pair announced they'd be fighting for the WBC belt in Las Vegas later this year. But even now, Fury couldn't resist firing a sly dig at Joshua, who'd failed in his talks over a unification fight with Wilder. Joshua was supposedly keen on unifying the heavyweight division, but would now fight WBA mandatory challenger Alexander Povetkin instead.

Many again commented that Eddie Hearn knew full well that Joshua had been lucky to sneak into the position of 'Number One' heavyweight via the back door, during Fury's hiatus. Fury certainly thought so.

[As a side note: There had once been an outside chance that Fury himself might have ended up in the Hearn stable. Back in the day, John Fury had been invited to reacquaint himself with Eddie Hearn's father, Barry (the well-known sports impresario and snooker overlord), someone he'd known from his days in pro boxing. When John arrived at the event in Newcastle, he saw that Barry was a little worse for wear. With John being teetotal, he realized that there was no meaningful conversation to be had and turned on his heels and left. So when Mick Hennessey approached the Fury camp, they signed with him instead, even though he was relatively inexperienced and had limited resources compared to many of the other promoters.]

Speaking of himself and Wilder, Fury observed...

> *We have two men who will fight anyone. He* [Wilder] *wanted to fight the biggest shithouse in the sport. This*

man has been trying to make a fight with another chump. AJ and Hearn have turned British boxing into a laughing stock

Wilder concurred, calling Fury, who was still boxing's lineal world heavyweight champion, 'a true champion'.

> I respect him and I salute him for accepting the fight in America, for trying to save face for his country, to try to save them from the embarrassment they feel over there. Because we're laughing at them hard, especially when Joshua asked for $50 million and then talked about he was just playing. But Fury, he's a true champion. This is what champions are all about. This is a bigger fight than the Joshua fight. This is a way bigger fight. Just for Tyson to take this opportunity, and be able to do a deal in a short amount of time, it tells you about his character. He's a true warrior. He's a true gypsy king and I can't wait to share a ring with him.
>
> This is humiliation for Joshua's side. They didn't wanna fight, they didn't wanna let me in the ring, they didn't want no confrontation with me, they didn't wanna look me in the eye. So we're showing the young boy what it is to be a man, what the requirements of this job are. So I hope Joshua and his team are taking

notes on what real champions are supposed to do. Real kings are supposed to fight each other. We are ready now. This fight we are having is on. This fight is official. It is on, baby. This is what we have been waiting for right here. The best fighting the best.

Promoter Frank Warren told the raucous sell-out crowd of 25,000 there'd be news the following week. 'All will be revealed next week, so wait for next week. But the fight is on. We are very advanced.'

No sooner had the words left his lips than the adrenaline-fuelled Tyson let slip that the fight would be held in Las Vegas, in November. Fury also confirmed that he would like to defend the WBC belt in Belfast if he successfully beat Wilder in the US. *'I promise you, I'm taking the WBC title and I'll bring it back and defend it right here in Belfast.'*

The *BT Sport* presenter had to apologize for Fury's language a second time when Fury promised that he *'would knock Wilder the fuck out'*.

Wilder was undefeated in 40 contests, with 39 knockouts. Joshua was undefeated in 21 contests. The prospect of two or three superfights between the trio of so-far unblemished boxers was raising the heavyweight division to a place it hadn't been for almost twenty-five years.

Round 11

Good Business

It turned out that Fury had already outwitted Joshua without even throwing a punch. While Joshua had dithered, Fury stole his thunder. No wonder, in the aftermath of the Pianeta fight, Fury planted a kiss on Wilder's cheek. And little wonder Wilder didn't object. And no wonder, too, that Frank Warren looked so pleased. There might be a fight in earnest in three months' time but, for the moment, they were partners in a very good piece of business.

No doubt equally pleased with the way things were panning out was one figure who hadn't climbed into the ring: Wilder's manager, Shelly Finkel — who'd worked for the best part of fifty years in boxing and the music industry with the likes of the Doors, Cream, and Mike Tyson. He knew a game-changer when he saw one — and that's exactly what Fury versus Wilder had now become. For the previous twenty years, heavyweight boxing in America had stagnated to the point of terminal decline. More recently, the biggest purses had involved fights at Wembley and Cardiff, where Joshua earned more per fight than Wilder did for his fights in the US. Finkel sensed an opportunity to create an American revival — and to bring back the 1990's-era of Mike Tyson, Evander Holyfield, and the rest.

* * *

It was almost a year previously, back in November 2017, that negotiations had first begun for a unification fight between Joshua and Wilder, but there'd been arguments over the division of the purse and rematch clauses. Finkel believed that Joshua and Hearn never really wanted a fight against Wilder anyway. In the meantime, Fury decided to make his return. It took nine months for the Joshua–Wilder talks to fail. It took less than two weeks for the Wilder-Fury match to be made — with the purse to be shared equally.

Over the next few months, Joshua would have to put up with the inevitable (and some would say justified) verbal abuse from Wilder and Fury, who would accuse him of ducking the fight, and of not being a true world champion, in view of the fact that he only ever fought on home soil. Once Wilder's power or Fury's skill had prevailed, Joshua would be bound to fight to unify all the titles. The clamour for the showdown would just keep growing — it would be irresistible. Sooner or later, Joshua would *surely* have to meet either Wilder or Fury on equal terms.

* * *

With no official announcement due until September, it seemed likely that Fury–Wilder would be held late November in either Las Vegas or New York. A promotional tour of major cities was planned.

Both Fury and Wilder were unbeaten, with impressive boxing credentials. Fury was a skilful but essentially defensive fighter. Wilder was the hardest hitter in the division, and possibly it's most dangerous man, with only one of his contests ever going the distance. As extravagant salesmen and self-promoters they were inseparable. But after the initial brouhaha, progress was slow; it took until the end of September for press conferences and promotion to start, as the fight was pushed forward to December, and the venue switched to the Los Angeles Staples Centre.

* * *

Though Joshua was still unbeaten, and still holder of three further versions of the world title, much to Eddie Hearn's chagrin Joshua was now third on the bill in terms of public interest and credibility. On 22 September, Joshua defended his titles — a mandatory contest ordered by the WBA — against Alexander Povetkin.

Just as happened against Klitschko, Joshua was matched against Povetkin at just the right time. The 37-year-old Russian was still a good fighter, but no longer a great fighter — age had caught up with him. Joshua had done an unprecedented level of stamina training for the fight and Povetkin knew that if he was going to win, he'd have to do it early. He started the better of the two fighters, taking the opening two rounds. Then a punch from the Russian left Joshua glassy-eyed and bloodied with a suspected broken nose.

But Joshua rode it out, and gradually found his range and rhythm, to land a powerful combination of punches that sent the Russian to the canvas. He only just beat the count and didn't look at all recovered. The referee let the fight go on for a few more seconds before the same happened again and the referee stepped in to end it. No-one had ever decked Povetkin like that in his entire career.

Immediately after Joshua's win, Eddie Hearn started talking about his next fight being in April 2019, against Dillian Whyte — the boxer he'd beaten the year previously for the British heavyweight title — though the camp claimed that a fight against Wilder was also on the cards. No mention was made of what might happen if Wilder didn't win his next fight. Fury wasn't slow in picking up on the fact that he'd wasn't even being mentioned as a potential opponent. He was on Instagram before Joshua had even wiped the sweat from his brow.

> *Safe to say that AJ and his team are a pack of shithouses and will rob the British boxing fans of Britain's biggest fight. They will never fight me ever. Way too slow and ponderous. Can't box eggs. Contact me when you grow a pair. I'm 27-0-19 and the lineal heavyweight champion of the world. Can't say I blame team Joshua.*

In a video post he added:

> *I think it's safe to say now that not Team Joshua or Matchroom Boxing will ever fight the Gypsy King. Never. They mentioned if it's not Wilder it'll be Whyte, no mention of Tyson Fury the lineal heavyweight champion of the world. It's alright you fighting men who are 39-years-old or half your size. Tonight is pure evidence that I'm fighting the best heavyweight out there in Deontay Wilder. Joshua is not even close. He is slow, methodical, and ponderous at times. Powerful yes, but they all are. It is obvious to see.*

Avoid me at all costs. If I were you, Anthony Joshua, I'd avoid me because I will jab your face off you bum. Can't box, jab your nut in, easy night's work. I've never seen a bigger bum in my life.

Eddie Hearn's feeble counter claim was that Fury wasn't being considered because he'd never been involved in an 'entertaining' fight.

All eyes were now on Wilder and Fury. But if Fury was to win in December, then Wilder would want a rematch, probably in early 2019, so a Fury fight in April would not be possible. Secondly, if Wilder were to win then he would still be the WBC champion — so the fight that would then make sense would be AJ v Wilder for the undisputed rights. The only way Fury would come into the picture was if he did the business and beat Wilder so convincingly that Wilder didn't want the rematch. Otherwise, Fury had to beat Wilder twice — while AJ fought Whyte — which would (with no mandatories coming into play) finally set the scene for the Fury v AJ fight sometime in late 2019 at the earliest.

* * *

With the Fury—Wilder fight confirmed for 1 December at the LA Staples Center, at the beginning of October the two fighters were in London for the first leg of a three-part promotional tour. They were guests on the ITV's *Good Morning Britian,* hosted by Piers Morgan and Susanna Reid, before they headed to a press conference in London — before heading to another in New York on Tuesday, and travelling on to Los Angeles the following day.

Just moments after sitting down, Fury unleashed a sensational, if predictable, rant towards Wilder. The pair continued to trade insults as Fury got up out of his seat and asked Wilder to demonstrate his punching power.

'Can we have a little spar now I want to feel the punching power,' he said, standing up as if making ready to fight.

The comments apparently infuriated Wilder so much he was forced to push the Fury in retaliation.

'My wife pushes harder than that you little bitch,' said Fury.

Unfortunately the smirk on Frank Warren's face gave the pantomime away.

The theatre that followed also had more than a hint of excess about it. After apparently being invited to show off his power on the Spanish language *Nación ESPN* channel, Deontay Wilder landed a huge right hand on a mascot wearing a sombrero and a moustache. And so we found out that a layer of packing foam doesn't, in fact, protect you from the WBC heavyweight champion punching you upside the head as hard as he can. Wilder claimed not to know that there was 'a human being' inside the costume. Early reports claimed that the recipient of the punch had suffered a broken jaw, but that turned out not to be the case. A 'contrite' Wilder offered the mascot tickets to the fight. Throughout the build-up, the knockabout stuff continued.

Closer to the fight, as tensions built, Wilder went on a deranged rant saying he's been asked racist questions in a presser. Meanwhile, Fury vowed to donate his entire '£8m purse' for the fight to the homeless — though that might have been a ploy to get people to check later what he'd done with his purse — as a way of it being seen that he'd got his full whack — after it was rumoured that he only actually got £1.5 million of the supposed £5m he was to receive from the Klitschko fight.

Even closer to the real business end of things — two weeks before the fight — trainer Ben Davison wasn't underestimating the task ahead: 'Deontay Wilder is the most dangerous fighter in world boxing — lightning quick, punches like a horse kicking — he's got a long reach. He's a very dangerous man.'

Fury and Wilder began to trade verbal barbs, as each looked to claim any advantage in the mind-games. Fury, by his standards, was unusually calm; Wilder upped the ante by questioning Fury's motives to move his training camp to Los

Angeles and bring in the renowned trainer Freddie Roach, who'd enjoyed an illustrious career working with the likes of Manny Pacquaio, Amir Khan, and Oscar De La Hoya.

Roach, 58, revealed his role in the camp, telling *Sports Illustrated* that Fury approached him to do his cuts on fight night. Wilder said it was evidence that Fury was getting 'nervous'. Fury countered that he'd been 'living rent-free in Wilder's mind for the past week'.

On 8 October — in a *BT Sport* promo piece — Wilder and Fury sat opposite each other. Fury fixed Wilder with an unblinking gaze:

> *This is a fight that everyone's gonna want to watch. And the reason is I'm not going to have to play tic-tac boxing. I'm coming home to destroy cruiserweights — and to me you're only a few pounds over cruiserweight limit. And when you feel eighteen-nineteen stone on the jaw — and you will feel it sooner or later — your defence is quite leaky — you throw wild punches — you're eager to land — I'll tag you — and when I tag you it's over. I'm not 40 years old, like Luis Ortiz. When I get going I will jump on you and get you out of there for sure. And when you start swinging — that's 'Welcome to my world' — that's 'Christmas come early'.*

No-one can land a swing on me — nobody — from any direction. Up and coming, round the corner, I see them all. So unless you're going to bring something I've not seen before, which is very unlikely... because I've watched all your fights and I know what you do — you look for them big wild punches. You haven't got a prayer.

Wilder sat, impassive and silent, and looked as if he was thinking, 'There's thirty-six minutes of boxing, and I only have to land *one* good shot.'

Round 12

Fury v Wilder

It was hard to know how this fight would play out. The power edge clearly belonged to Wilder — he was the kind of fighter who could suddenly end a fight against *any* opponent in the world. But he was also prone to getting wild when releasing that power, throwing crazy windmill punches at times and abandoning all defence. The technique edge clearly went to Fury — a crafty and tricky fighter who walked into the Klitschko fight with a near-perfect game plan, which he executed beautifully. He wouldn't get suckered into a shoot-out with Wilder, and would surely use his movement — if he could keep it up for twelve rounds.

He did that against Klitschko — but that was three years earlier, and Klitschko was a lot slower than Wilder. The feeling was that there'd be a slow first few rounds where Fury dodged and frustrated Wilder, scoring points, followed by

Wilder starting to get a bit desperate. And that's more or less how it began — but what happened in the end, not even a Hollywood script could've imagined

* * *

Round 1: The fighters are in the centre of the ring, measuring each other up. Those awful 'USA! USA!' chants start from half the crowd. Wilder feints, Fury mocks him. Wilder lands a jab, but Fury puts his hands behind his back, baiting Wilder. Both have their moments but the round goes to Fury.

10-9, Fury.

Round 2: Fury looks more comfortable in the second. He throws a few jabs and is moving well. Now he's clowning again, throwing his hands skyward to bait Wilder. Wilder charges in, but Fury wraps him up. Not much lands that round apart from a good right hand from Wilder at the end of the round. Another close round that could be called either way, but we'll give it to Wilder.

19-19

Round 3: Wilder's not used to fighting opponents who move this well — because there aren't any others like Fury at heavyweight. Fury's head movement and feinting are good, keeping the American off-balance and tentative. Wilder lands a nice left hook to the body, but Fury is scoring upstairs with his jab. Wilder swings wildly with a right and Fury responds back with a quick flurry of pot-shots to the belly. It's the clearest round yet.

29-28, Fury

Round 4: Fury is moving really well now; but can he keep it up for twelve rounds? Wilder misses again with a right, as Fury counters with a hook. Fury connects with a series of jabs. Wilder misses yet again with another big right — he's missing with so many big right hands! Fury's is the more impressive boxing, but when Wilder *does* land he's landing the heavier

punches. There's a trickle of blood from Fury's nose. A closer round again, but it goes to Fury.

39-37, Fury

Round 5: Fury is using his left jab so well — as range finder, attacking weapon, and defensive barricade. But he's slackening off a bit. Is stamina going to be issue? Wilder is still missing and now his eye is beginning to swell. It's a continuing theme, Fury scoring with jabs and Wilder missing. Will he be able to stay clear of that Wilder right if he begins to fade? In the dying seconds Wilder tries to steal a very close round with a big one-two combo as he walks Fury into a corner, but both shots miss by a distance. Another close round to Fury — but he needs to do more than make Wilder miss.

49-46, Fury

Round 6: Fury backs Wilder down with a combination. He's busy again and Wilder looks tentative. Fury is controlling entire stretches of the fight with his jab. Wilder lands a few clean lefts toward the end of the round, including one good sharp one. We're only halfway through the scheduled twelve rounds distance and Wilder is already in trouble on the scorecards — already needing something special to win.

59-55, Fury

Round 7: Wilder's eye is swelling, but Fury's face is also bearing several patches of bruising contact now. It's obvious

Wilder has no Plan B — and probably never has had. He's just hoping to land ONE BIG SHOT, but so far it's not happening. A big right hand over the top scores for Fury! Now Wilder appears to have landed as Fury falls backward and the American comes to life, swinging wildly at Fury who is backed along the ropes. But Fury smartly wraps his opponent up and stems the flow. This is looking bad for Wilder. Fury is just making him miss everything and doing enough to win the rounds.

69-64, Fury

Round 8: This is turning into a boxing lesson by Fury, who continues to showboat. Wilder is being exposed and it doesn't seem like he or his corner has any answers. Wilder needs a knockdown.

79-73, Fury

Round 9: Wilder finally lands his big right hand and down goes Fury in a heap! Fury is down in the 9th! He beats the count and wraps Wilder up as he tries to barrel in for the finish. Now we've got a fight! Suddenly Wilder looks like he's hurt! Both men are exhausted. What a round! Wilder pulls back two points.

87-83, Fury

Round 10: Amazingly, astonishingly, Fury looks to have completely recovered. He lands a big right on Wilder early in the round and is once again throwing his left jab with authority, coming forward with it, doubling it up, even tripling it up. Wilder badly needed that knockdown, but it's almost as if Fury did, too, to bring this out of him. Wilder seems a bit punched out from the last round. He's not throwing much here. Fury misses with a big left-right combo. Good rally by Wilder at the end but not enough. What a response from Fury.

97-92, Fury

Round 11: Fury continues to jab away, still boxing so well — making Wilder miss again and again with clever head and upper-body movement, coolly picking his shots in response. Wilder still needs a knockout. Wilder's power bailed him out when he was out-boxed by Szpilka and Ortiz, but can it bail him out here? A good left hook by Wilder but it's not enough.

107-101, Fury

Round 12:
Fury is down again!
Early in the 12th!
Hit twice!
A right— and a perfectly-timed left!
That's it!
...He's not going to beat the count!

Tyson Fury is flat on his back, his eyes staring into blinding light, like a patient waking on an operating table — like a man having a near-death experience. Across the other side of the ring, Deontay Wilder draws a hand slowly across his throat. It's over. The fight is done. He's hit plenty of opponents like that before. He knows how it ends. It's ended.

Yet, somehow ...*somehow!* Fury's eyes are open, but we can only wonder at what he's seeing... It's as if the last three years of his life have suddenly reversed and compressed into three seconds — and then somehow run fast forward and unravelled again as a deep in-breath shudders through him. *Inspiration!* Like one of those supernatural-movie characters that can't be killed, Fury makes it to his feet! *Somehow!* He just beats the count and the referee lets him continue. Fury is hanging on for dear life! Unbelievable! Two minutes left! Tyson Fury is just two minutes away from completing a truly miraculous comeback from the abyss. Wilder goes in for the finish but Fury prevails — and then comes on stronger landing more shots of his own. And there's the bell! What a round!

Final score: Fury 115-Wilder 111

Throughout the fight, Fury had alternately dropped his hands to goad Wilder, and then used his hands to keep him at bay, catching him flush on several occasions. When Wilder finally connected, Fury punched himself on his own head to show that he could take more. Yes, he was knocked down twice, but by then Wilder's eyes were swollen, and his legs had turned to jelly. Everyone saw that Fury had done enough to win.

But the judges didn't see it that way and forced a split decision — with Alejandro Rochin awarding the fight to *Wilder* by 115-111! Canadian Robert Tapper gives it to Fury (114-112); and UK judge Phil Edwards has them tied on 113-113.

Tellingly — as an embarrassed-looking referee raised both fighters' hands — it was Wilder who was most happy and relieved, and Fury's camp who were visibly baffled and disappointed — along with millions of others. Among the many who felt that Fury had been robbed was Floyd Mayweather. Per Andreas Hale, the Senior Editor of *Sporting News*, stood in front of the ring shaking his head in disbelief at Fury as the scores were announced.

Even before the result was announced a couple of 'high-profile' people from the Wilder camp had gone over to the Fury camp and said: 'Great performance. Don't worry; we'll get him in the rematch.'

Fury's trainer, Ben Davison could only comment, 'To ruin the biggest comeback in boxing history — that is a disgrace. You've got to be a sick person to do that someone.'

At the same time, social media was awash with comments, most of them fairly brief and direct...

- I've seen better decisions on *16 and Pregnant*.
- Wow! The judges just ruined the biggest fight of the year.
- That was never a fucking draw. Bullshit.
- Not only is it not a draw, now I don't even win my bet.

Boxers and ex-boxers added their own comments...

Lennox Lewis: 'This Wilder-Fury judging takes me back to my first fight with Holyfield. [It] just goes to show how hard it is for a Brit to come to America and take someone's belt, even though that's what we clearly saw. 'Big up' to Tyson Fury, who never ceases to amaze me. Hold your head high! ...I just saw Tyson Fury come back from drugs, depression, two years of inactivity, and massive weight loss to outbox the WBC heavyweight champion. In a rematch, I can only imagine that he will be even better prepared.

Trainer Dave Coldwell tweeted: 'I gave Wilder two 10-8s and one other round. That's it. Fury was brilliant tonight and the only man that looked like a winner.'

Andre Ward: 'A draw, I can understand (even though I feel Fury won by two or three rounds). With two knockdowns and a round here or there for Wilder, you have a draw in some people's eyes. But 115-111 for Wilder is terrible, just terrible!! That's what's wrong with boxing. Fury's stock went up!!!!!'

Tony Bellew: 'Boxing is the biggest loser with decisions like that! The last round makes it closer but it's still a win for Fury in my eyes! Still, there's a growing sense in the sport that these results are being orchestrated just to fill everyone's pockets.'

Chris Eubank Jr: 'For anyone confused about the draw. It's simple maths. A draw = Rematch. A Rematch = Dollars.'

* * *

Tyson Fury had fought bravely and with class, better than anyone could have possibly imagined or expected. He fought technically and tactically. Everything he did had a purpose, even when he appeared to be playing the fool. It was an intelligent and agile performance against a dangerous fighter in his prime. Yes, he played the showman, but not the clown. He grinned, dropped his hands, held them up, put them behind his back, and kept up a constant verbal stream directed at Wilder as Fury's slightly quivering frame poked its own fun, at Wilder's athletic tone. Fury taunted and tricked him, and made him miss so many times. It was Fury's version of 'rope-a-dope' to anger Wilder, to make him punch himself dry.

'Look at me!' he was saying. 'Look at this. You can't get near me. But you can't lay a glove on me, can you?'

And even when Wilder did get through – in the ninth and again in the final round – Fury's resilience was outrageous. He could take the biggest punches that the heavyweight division had to offer, and this night proved it. He could avoid them, too. The judge that scored the fight to Wilder could only have been impressed by his aggression, because his accuracy was terrible.

By Wilder's own admission, he got too emotional and forgot his game plan — he just wanted Fury gone and, in his emotional state, lost sight of his own game plan. When the moment came for the final big bomb, Wilder simply didn't have it left in him. He was no longer focussed, he couldn't hit the target, he didn't have the power to put Fury down a third time. He had been out-boxed, and was all boxed out. So he didn't win. But he didn't lose either, this being the most frustrating of split decisions: a draw.

Fury took on Wilder, the most explosively dangerous puncher in the world, as a brave gamble. It was one that paid off handsomely. A rematch was what everyone wanted. And, for the time being, Anthony Joshua now found himself a support act in heavyweight boxing's biggest show. Fury didn't lose the opportunity to taunt him with a comical squawking impersonation, saying, 'There's one other heavyweight around but he's ...CHICKEN!'

> *Joshua did not want this fight, and he did not want it because Wilder is one of the fiercest punchers in heavyweight history. I know that because I felt it tonight. AJ didn't want no part of that right hand, let me tell you. He can't move like me. He would have been nailed. He couldn't have got out of the way of Wilder. No way.*

Later, Frank Warren added his own comments:

> We know about the fighters who look like they're sculpted out of marble who can't fight. There's something in you if you're a fighter. Yes, physically you've got to be strong. You've got to have a good engine. He [Fury] showed that in the fight with Wilder. When he went down — when he hit the deck — I thought it was all over. Wilder's people jumped up — they thought they'd lost the fight until then.
>
> I don't believe that Joshua wants to fight Fury, but I think he's being shamed into it. Tyson Fury has gone from nowhere — gone from Brick Lane to Park Lane — in a very short space of time. He's come back from a terrible abyss that he got himself into. He's got himself

back on track and the British public like someone who has been on the ground and come back. And he's shown tremendous heart after he got cheated in that fight in America. He's overtaken Anthony Joshua as far as the British public is concerned. Does Anthony Joshua bring more to the table than Tyson Fury? The answer to that is no. Are the Hearns scared of this fight? Yes... because he'll lose. Eddie Hearn is astute enough to know that if his cash cow goes then, hang on a minute, where's the next one coming from?

Most people might now concur that Joshua and his manager would dodge Fury and Wilder for as long as they could — maybe taking meaningless side fights with the likes of Dillian Whyte. Eddie Hearn's feeble claim was that Fury had never been considered as an opponent for Joshua, because he'd never been in an 'entertaining' fight, had been blown clean out of the water.

For the first time after a decade-and-a-half of Klitschko's best Dalek impersonations, we'd seen a great fight between two heavyweights. For the first time in a long time, the top of the division had quality and excitement. There's a saying, 'As goes the heavyweight division, so goes boxing'. So it had been a great night. ...A man who could punch like that — and a man who could box like that!

* * *

Was Fury robbed? Wilder reckoned that his two 10-8 knockdown rounds did enough and a draw was a fair result. Fury thought he'd won the fight by completely out-boxing Wilder. Wilder countered that referee Jack Weiss had been slow to make the ten count in the last round, while Fury was gazing into space.

'I don't know how he got up,' said Wilder. 'I don't know why they didn't start the count earlier. I really thought I had him out of there. I got heavy hands and I hit hard. I saw his eyes roll back in his head, I saw Jack on the ground checking him, and I thought, "It's over." Only God knows how he got back up. Fury was laid out, but they hesitated.'

Fury's own post-fight complaints were philosophical and PR savvy, rather than bitter, and ensured peace reigned at the Staples Center, despite the many thousands in the loud and boisterous travelling contingent. Had Fury turned nasty in the aftermath, they might have too. One word from him and they would likely have trashed the place. Instead he offered another of his impromptu songs: *American Pie*.

> *It was an excellent fight, I had a great dance partner ... Thinking about it would only make me hold grudges against people, and I'm not here to hold*

grudges against anyone. I'm still alive and well, and that's the most important thing.

Fury responded to Wilder claim that he'd put him through hell...

If that's hell, then it's not a very scary place. I had fun in there. Yeah, he's the hardest puncher in the world, but you don't really feel the punches when you're in a fight. I think the adrenaline's pumping so much and you're in the moment, that you don't really feel them till the next day.

The morning after the fight, while he still looked 'marked' but not 'damaged', Fury gave a short interview. He was still his usual garrulous self, and only gave himself away right at the end when he voice broke with the emotion of what he'd just said....

I had two and half years out of the ring... ten stone ballooned... mental health problems... I just showed the world tonight... everyone suffering with mental health... you can come back, and it can be done. Everybody out there who has the same problems that I've been suffering with, I did that for your guys. You know the truth — everybody knows I won that fight. And if I can come back from where I came from, then you can do it too. So get up. Get over it. Seek help. And let's do it together as a team. I did it for you guys.

* * *

Fury's wiser and calmer responses meant that he and Wilder would now 'dance' again. If Fury maintained his impressive training regime, he might be even fitter and better prepared, and have even more of an edge.

Wilder's manager, Shelly Finkel, disagreed: 'The next time Wilder fights, he will be better. I don't know if Fury can be better. I give him all the credit in the world for getting up. It would have been easy not to. So I think while you saw the best of Fury, you did not see the best of Wilder.'

Fury had now beaten the best, twice — supposedly vastly-superior opponents, — in two massive title fights. People *really* wanted to see Fury again, now — and not just his home crowd but in America too. Joshua was no longer top dog. Though it had been a draw in Los Angeles, you couldn't help feeling that Fury had won. While he left empty-handed, he had silenced the critics of his comeback and could go into any rematch full of confidence. Fury was back, and everyone knew it.

With this showing Fury dispelled any myths that his win over Klitschko was a one-off. For most people, he'd now added Wilder's scalp to his record, and when he went on to beat Joshua, that would be the three best heavyweights of his generation beaten.

* * *

Few people could have anticipated the waves made by the fight that had just happened — except those who are somehow offered a glimpse of destiny. The sporting world had suddenly to catch hold of a drama that had been building for years.

Maybe the story had begun when Tyson Fury tore down the monolith called Klitschko, and then returned — an outrageous victor — to a public of indifference and hostility, and a series of events that jeopardized his career indefinitely. Others might look further back to the time when an Olympic champion-in-waiting was humbled by Fury during a sparring session — a day that still leaves Anthony Joshua's corner wincing. And all the while a third, older, man, Deontay Wilder, was forging his own way, toppling challengers as he hit out towards his own goals.

After Wilder v Fury, many commentators changed tack and suddenly 'recognized' Fury's unique brilliance. Fury, Wilder, and Joshua were now being spoken about almost like the components of a game of stone-scissors-paper. Which one would beat the other? Would the Fury–Wilder rematch happen? Who would fight Joshua first? When, and where? There was talk of trying to stage a Fury-Joshua title fight in Nigeria — another *Rumble in the Jungle* — *Lightning in Lagos*. We were faced with a scenario unprecedented in sporting history — with three undefeated heavyweight 'world champions' who were all approaching their peak years. Who would emerge supreme? It was a new destiny that not even Tyson Fury himself could have imagined or anticipated.

* * *

Tyson Fury announced that he'd be donating the purse for his recent fight to homeless charities after he'd been shocked by the number of people he'd seen on the streets of Los Angeles. He made good his promise and confirmed it later, when a fan asked him about his pledge during the Q&A segment of a charity auction in Cardiff in February 2019.

> *I did give away my last purse, but I don't do charity work for a pat on the back. I do it to help people, but I don't want praise for it, I don't want to be called a do-gooder ... Money comes, money goes — you blow it like a runny nose!*

Why then did he give away millions to the homeless yet still haggle about money?

> *...Because I don't want people to underestimate my intelligence.'*

Fury was as good as his word and donated his entire purse to several UK charities specializing in providing housing for recovering alcoholics and addicts. Though his actual purse for the fight was about $3.5 million, with the pay-per-view income added, his total payment amounted to roughly $9 million – all of which he gave away.

* * *

The biggest thing about Tyson Fury has never been his size — but his personality. When he speaks, you know that nothing is pre-planned. It's freestyle — all off-the-cuff. It's the same in the ring — free-wheeling, big but agile, orthodox or southpaw. He's a true one-off. His fortunes, like his fists, have swung in all directions — his moods have always swung just as rapidly. Sometimes he speaks non-stop about other boxers; at other times he refuses to say a word. There is a sense that he still struggles to find calmness and stability, when the only career open to him is one that depends on show-stopping action.

When his next opponent gets into the ring he will face the same questions that any interviewer or follower of boxing asks himself: 'Which Fury has turned up today?' The one who said he wished he'd never heard about boxing? ...Or the man who said he wants to go on and beat Joe Louis' record? The one who gives his prize purse to the homeless? ...Or the one who asks a biographer, *'What's in it for me?'* And the fact is he can be many people at once. Serious jester. Heroic villain.

* * *

From the mid-80s to the mid-90s, great heavyweights came around so often that, in the case of Ali, Frazier, and Foreman, their careers overlapped. Mike Tyson was a great heavyweight, and Evander Holyfield and Lennox Lewis were more than respectable. And then the well suddenly ran dry. The world heavyweight division atrophied under the ubiquitous Klitschko, as a succession of British boxers underwhelmed — Audley Harrison, David Price, Dereck Chisora. Attention went elsewhere — to lighter skilful boxers like Floyd Mayweather, or to the more-showy MMA arena — and eventually to farces like Mayweather versus the MMA champion, Conor McGregor. Along with Joshua and Wilder, Fury has made heavyweight boxing engaging again. And this is one of the reasons that we engage with him.

Boxing — and, in particular, heavyweight boxing — has never been purely about fighting. The redemption story, which could hang itself so neatly on Fury's tale, has already been branded by Joshua — the youth who was once arrested and fitted with an electronic tag — but who now has major sponsors, an OBE, and a reputation as the likeable face of boxing. Against that, Fury still remains a bad boy who sponsors are more reticent about. Back in the day, Jack Johnson's story was about race and equality. Muhammad Ali's story virtually transcends what it means to be human.

Tyson Fury's own story is one that brings out the light and the shadow sides of human nature. He will continue to live his life on a daily basis, unconcerned with what you, or I, or anyone else thinks of him — a subscriber to the motto: *'Opinions are like arse holes — everybody's got one.'*

I don't look at this as a comeback.
Because I'm not coming back to what I once was.
This is a new me.
This is a new Tyson Fury.
This is a new book.
I'm not going to rewrite the old story.
That book's finished.
It never, ever, ever was opened again.
The legacy of Tyson Fury, from being a child to being the heavyweight champion of his dreams — that book has been closed.

This is a new book...

To be continued....

Tyson Fury: At A Glance

Born: 12 August 1988

Birth Name: Tyson Luke Fury

Alias: Gyspy King

Hometown: Wilmslow, Cheshire

Country: Irish / English

Birthplace: Wythenshawe, Manchester

Division: Heavyweight

Stance: Orthodox (but switches)

Weight: 18 ½ stones / 258 pounds / 117 kilos

Height: 6 foot 9 inches / 2.09 metres

Reach: 85 inches / 216 cm

Manager: Frank Warren

Trainer: Ben Davison

Professional Record: 27 wins (19 by knockout) – 0 defeats – 1 draw

Amateur Career

As an amateur, in 2006, Tyson Fury won bronze at the AIBA Youth World Boxing Championships. In England, in the same year, representing Jimmy Egan's Boxing Academy, he took part in the senior national championships but was beaten by David Price 22–8.

Fury represented both Ireland and England. Initially fighting out of the Holy Family Boxing Club in Belfast in the North, later switching to the Smithboro Club in Monaghan in the Republic, he represented Ireland three times at international level.

In an international competition against an experienced Polish team, in 2007, the Irish team lost 12–6 overall — though Fury himself was victorious in both his bouts, in Rzeszów and Białystok. In a later Irish match, against a US team, Fury won his bout by KO.

He was forced to withdraw from the Irish National Championships after officials from the Holy Trinity Boxing Club in West Belfast (the club of the-then amateur heavyweight champion) submitted a protest regarding his eligibility.

As a junior, Fury was ranked World #3 behind the Russians, Maxim Babanin, and Andrey Volkov,

In May 2007, representing England, he won the EU Junior Championship, but later lost to Maxim Babanin in the final — and then lost out to David Price for a place at the 2008 Beijing Olympics representing the UK. Fury also tried unsuccessfully to qualify for Ireland. But instead of waiting four years for a chance that might not come anyway, Fury forgot about the Olympics and turned professional.

In 2008, (in the absence of Price, who went on to win bronze in Beijing) Fury became the ABA National Champion.

Tyson Fury's amateur record is: 31 wins — 26 by KO — with 4 defeats.

Professional Boxing Record

6 Dec 2008
> v Béla Gyöngyösi (Hungary)
> National Ice Centre, Nottingham, England.
> Professional debut
> WON / TKO / Round 1 of 6 / 2:14

17 Jan 2009
> v Marcel Zeller (Germany)
> DW Stadium, Wigan, England
> WON / TKO / Round 3 of 6 / 2:50

28 Feb 2009
> v Daniil Peretyatko (Russia)
> Showground, Norwich, England
> WON / TKO / Round 2 of 6 / 3:00

14 Mar 2009
> v Lee Swaby (UK)
> Aston Events Centre, Birmingham, England
> WON / TKO / Round 4 of 6 / 3:00

11 Apr 2009
> v Matthew Ellis (UK)
> York Hall, London, England
> WON / KO / Round 1 of 6 / 0:48

23 May 2009
> Scott Belshaw (UK)
> Colosseum, Watford, England
> WON / TKO / Round 2 of 8 / 0:52

18 Jul 2009
> v Aleksandrs Selezens (Latvia)
> York Hall, London, England
> WON / TKO/ Round 3 of 6 / 0:48

11 Sep 2009
> v John McDermott (UK)
> Brentwood Centre Arena, Brentwood, England
> Won English heavyweight title
> WON / Referee's Points Decision: 98-92 / Round 10

26 Sep 2009
> v Tomas Mrazek (Czech Republic)
> O2 Arena, Dublin, Ireland
> WON / Points Decision / Round 6

5 Mar 2010
> v Hans-Joerg Blasko (Germany)
> Leisure Centre, Huddersfield, England
> WON / TKO / Round 1of 8 / 2:14

25 Jun 2010
    v John McDermott (UK)
    Brentwood Centre Arena, Brentwood, England
    Won vacant English heavyweight title
    WON / TKO / Round 9 of 12 / 1:08

10 Sep 2010
    v Rich Power (USA)
    York Hall, London, England
    WON / Points Decision / Round 8

19 Dec 2010
    Zack Page (USA)
    Colisée Pepsi, Quebec City, Quebec, Canada
    WON / Unanimous Decision / Round 8

19 Feb 2011
    v Marcelo Luiz Nascimento (Brazil)
    Wembley Arena, London, England
    WON / KO / Round 5 of 10 / 2:48

23 Jul 2011
    v Dereck Chisora (UK)
    Wembley Arena, London, England
    Won British and Commonwealth heavyweight titles
    WON / Unanimous Decision: 117–112, 117–112, 118–11 / Round   12

18 Sep 2011
    v Nicolai Firtha (USA)
    King's Hall, Belfast, Northern Ireland
    WON / TKO / Round 5 of 12 / 2:19

12 Nov 2011
    v Neven Pajkic (Canada)
    EventCity, Manchester, England
    Retained Commonwealth heavyweight title
    WON / TKO / Round 3 of 12 / 2:44

14 Apr 2012
    v Martin Rogan (UK)
    Odyssey Arena, Belfast, Northern Ireland
    Won vacant Irish heavyweight title
    WON / TKO / Round 5 of 12 / 3:00

7 Jul 2012
    v Vinny Maddalone (USA)
    Hand Arena, Clevedon, England
    Won vacant WBO Inter-Continental heavyweight title
    WON / TKO / Round 5 of 12 / 1:35

1 Dec 2012
    v Kevin Johnson (USA)
    Odyssey Arena, Belfast, Northern Ireland
    WON / Unanimous Decision: 119-110, 119-108, 119-108 / Round 12

20 Apr 2013
    v Steve Cunningham (USA)
    Madison Square Garden, New York City, USA
    WON / KO / Round 7 of 12 / 2:55

15 Feb 2014
    v Joey Abell (USA)
    Copper Box Arena, London, England
    WON / TKO / Round 4 of 10 / 1:48

29 Nov 2014
    v Dereck Chisora
    ExCeL Arena, London, England
    Won European, WBO International, vacant British heavyweight titles
    WON / Retired / Round 10 of 12 / 3:00

28 Feb 2015
    v Christian Hammer (Romania)
    The O2 Arena, London, England
    Retained WBO International heavyweight title
    WON / Retired / Round 8 of 12 / 3:00

28 Nov 2015
    v Wladimir Klitschko (Ukraine)
    Esprit Arena, Düsseldorf, Germany
    Won WBA (Super), IBF, WBO, IBO, *The Ring*, and lineal heavyweight titles
    WON / Unanimous Decision: 116-111, 115-112, 115-112 / Round 12

* * *

9 June 2018
>   v Sefer Seferi (Albania)
>   Manchester Arena, England
>   WON / Retired / Round 4 of 10 / 3.00

18 August 2018
>   v Francesco Pianeta (Italy)
>   Windsor Park, Belfast
>   WON / Referee's Points Decision 100/90 / Round 10

1 December 2018
>   v Deontay Wilder (USA)
>   Staples Center, Los Angeles
>   DRAW / 111-115, 114.112, 113-113

References

Sandhu, Nathan. 'No gloves, no licence, but plenty of blood.' Daily Mirror. 9 March 2018.

'Tyson Fury on Abell, Chisora, Johnson, Klitschko, and Retirement'. iFL TV. 13 Februrary 2014.

Wilson, Scott. 'Tyson Fury explains why his win over Wladimir Klitschko was better than Anthony Joshua's.' Give Me Sport. 2018.

'A 25-year-old single mum has revealed embarrassing details about her affair with new heavyweight boxing champion Tyson Fury.' The Sun (Australia) December 15 2015.

Rucki, Alexandra. 'Tyson Fury is a dad for the fourth time... and he's keeping up the tradition of unusual names.' Manchester Evening News. 4 December 2017.

Lutz, Tom. 'Tyson Fury beats Wladimir Klitschko: world heavyweight boxing – as it happened.' The Guardian. 28 November 2015.

'Tyson Fury in unlikely partnership with snooker legend Ronnie O'Sullivan ahead of comeback fight.' The Independent. 18 May 2018.

Bonner, Stayton. 'World Heavyweight Champion Tyson Fury: "I've Done Lots of Cocaine."' Rolling Stone, 4 October 2016.

Evans, Tom. 'Kickboxing star who spars with Tyson Fury claims Gypsy King would SCHOOL Anthony Joshua.' Daily Star. 25 May 2018.

Warren, Frank. 'Tyson Fury is back and journey to return titles starts now.' Daily Star. 14 April 2018.

Green, Simon. 'Tyson Fury HAILED by boxing fans for cutting off awkward interview.' Daily Star. 13 April 2018.

Bhambra, Pav. John Fury Interview. PSB Sports. 12 April 2018.

'Lennox Lewis: "Tyson Fury is the man in the heavyweight division."' iFL TV. 13 July 2016.

'Hilarious outcome when Fury telephoned Joshua to arrange their fight.' Boxing News Channel. 6 May 2018.

Warrington, Declan. 'Tyson Fury to face Sefer Seferi in next month's comeback fight.' The Independent. 20 May 2018.

'Tyson Fury says comeback bout against Sefer Seferi will be no easy task.' Sky Sports Boxing News. 30 May 2018.

Jones, Stephen. '"He's like a new boy": Tyson Fury chat leaves youngster delighted.' The Irish News. 22 January 2018.

Reddy, Luke. 'Tyson Fury v Sefer Seferi: The return, Joshua-Wilder targets and Ricky Hatton in awe.' BBC Sport Boxing. 9 June 2018.

Rafael, Dan. 'Tyson Fury signs with management company MTK Global.' ESPN. 25 November 2017.

Downes, Wally. 'HE'S BACK Tyson Fury should fight Tony Bellew on route to biggest fight in history with Anthony Joshua.' The Sun. 12 April 2018.

Robertson, Alexander. 'Tyson Fury "buys Nando's for all 52 diners at restaurant costing £700" after finishing a training session ahead of comeback fight.' Mail Online. 7 June 2018.

Khan, Issan. '"When he walked through the door, I predicted he'd be heavyweight world champion": Tyson Fury's first boxing coach on how a gangly 6ft 14-year-old made it to the top.' Mail Online. 9 June 2018.

Powell, Jeff. 'Frank Warren believes Tyson Fury will prove himself "the greatest heavyweight of his generation" ahead of the Gipsy King's comeback fight.' Daily Mail. 7 June 2018.

Matthews, Daniel. 'Tyson Fury hopes to surpass Joe Louis' record of 25 world heavyweight title defences: "If anyone is capable, I am."' Mail Online. 20 March 2018.

'Everyone wants to see the big fight': Deontay Wilder hints at wanting to take on Anthony Joshua or Tyson Fury next as he gears up for May 18 bout with Dominic Breazeale in New York

Rai, Radjvir. 'Tyson Fury: I'd be dead or in jail without boxing... it's like a drug, but you can never be cured.' Mail Online. 25 July 2014.

Forrester, Richard. Atkins, Stuart. 'Tyson Fury "treats himself to a new mansion" and poses beside massive columns at the property believed to be in Spain.' Sun. 9 February 2018.

Drake, Matthew. 'Tyson Fury mentor uncle was drug crime baron who ran amphetamine empire from inside jail.' Mirror. 4 February 2016.

Hutchinson, John. 'Tyson Fury announces retirement from boxing and blasts his uncle Peter Fury for visiting fierce rival David Haye's gym.' Sun. 31 July 2017.

'Tyson Fury next opponent REVEALED.' Boxing News. 12 July 2018.

Austin, Jack. 'Deontay Wilder vs Tyson Fury set for November as WBC champion hits out at "embarrassing" Anthony Joshua.' The Independent. 3 August 2018.

McKenzie, Mikael. 'Anthony Joshua mocked by Tyson Fury as Deontay Wilder fight confirmed.' Express. 19 August 2018.

Davies, Gareth A. Zeqiri, Daniel. 'Tyson Fury fight with Deontay Wilder "is on" after Gypsy King eases past Francesco Pianeta on points in Belfast. The Telegraph. 19 August 2018.

Winters, Max. 'Deontay Wilder shoves Tyson Fury in heated press conference...' Mail Online. 1 October 2018.

'Tyson Fury and His Wife Living Large.' Es News. 9 February 2018.

Smith, Matthew 'Deontay Wilder brands Anthony Joshua a coward...' Mail Online. 1 October 2018.

Taylor, Declan. 'Fury vs Wilder: Fight NOT sanctioned...' Daily Star. 10 October 2018.

Kershaw, Tom. 'Tyson Fury reveals depression almost led him to taking his own life.' Independent. 26 October 2018.

Morgan. Spencer. 'Tyson Fury opens up on his battle of depression.' Mail Online. 26 October 2018.

'Deontay Wiler absolutely loses it in Interview.' iFL TV. 28 November 2018.

Forrester, Richard. Atkins, Stuart. 'Generous Gypsy.' Sun. 26 November 2018.

Graham, Bryan Armen. 'Deontay Wilder retains WBC heavyweight title by split draw with Tyson Fury.' Guardian. 2 December 2018.

Frakes, Nicholas. 'That was NEVER a f***ing draw.' Express. 2 December 2018.

Sidle, Ryan. 'Tyson Fury Calls Anthony Joshua A Chicken After Controversial Draw.' Sport Bible. 2 December 2018.

'Everybody Who Watched the Fight Knows I've Won.' itv Good Morning Britain. 3 December 2018.

Fraser, Stuart. 'Greg Rutherford reveals extent of 'bedroom-hopping' at major athletics championships.' Mail Online. 27 October 2016.

'Klitschko Sauna Story.' Below the Belt with Brendan Schaub. 29 October 2018.

Caple, Alex. 'Tyson Fury details how he'd comfortably beat Anthony Joshua if they squared off.' Give Me Sport. 2018.

Hopcraft, George. 'Tyson Fury sends hilarious rematch message to Deontay Wilder' Give Me Sport. February 2019.

Lewis, Alex. 'Frank Warren reveals Tyson Fury's fight plans for 2019.' Give Me Sport. February 2019.

'Champion Boxer Donates Entire $9 Million Purse from Big Fight to House the Homeless' KindaKind. 11 February 2019.

Winehouse, Amitai. 'If that's hell, it's not a very scary place.' Mail Online. 7 March 2019

Photos

Front Cover: Jan Kruger / Getty Images (edited)

Cover Design & Artwork: Author

Page 16: Still from the documentary 'Knuckle': Gary Ashe / Allpix

Page 23: alamy

Page 25: Paris Fury / Twitter

Page 32: alamy

Page 39: Christopher Thomond / Observer

Page 51: Julian Finney / Getty Images

Page 59: BBC

Page 66: sports photo gallery

Page 69: Reuters

Page 83: scoopnest

Page 116: Irish Times

Page 124: Peter Fury / Twitter

Page 129: Ben Davison / Instagram

Page 135: YouTube

Page 153: ITV

Page 175: Reuters

Page 179: AP / Mark J Terrell

Page 181: boxingscene.com

Printed in Great Britain
by Amazon